## American Book Company
### The Standards Experts

# ACT® READING TEST
# PREPARATION GUIDE

### July 2008

**Rob Hunter**
**Jason Kirk**
**Zuzana Urbanek, Project Coordinator**
**Dr. Frank J. Pintozzi, Executive Editor**

**Contributing Writers:**
**Michelle Gunter, Dennis Martin**

**AMERICAN BOOK COMPANY**
**PO BOX 2638**
**WOODSTOCK, GEORGIA 30188-1383**
Toll Free: 1 (888) 264-5877   Phone: 770-928-2834
Toll Free Fax: 1 (866) 827-3240
Web site: www.americanbookcompany.com

# ACKNOWLEDGEMENTS

The authors would like to gratefully acknowledge the technical contributions of Marsha Torrens and Yvonne Benson and to thank Yvonne Benson for her work with the graphics in this book.
The authors also thank Mary Stoddard for the original icon.

The authors greatly appreciate the editing and proofreading expertise of Mallory Grantham.

Many thanks to those who contributed resource materials for the completion of this book, including Kindred Howard, Katie Semancik, Liz Thompson, and Emily Powell.

ACT® is a registered trademark of ACT, Inc. American Book Company is not affiliated with ACT, Inc., and produced this book independently.

©2009 American Book Company
PO Box 2638
Woodstock, GA 30188-1318

## ALL RIGHTS RESERVED

The text of this publication, or any part thereof, may not be reproduced or transmitted in any form or by any means, electronic or mechanical, including photocopying, recording, storage in an information retrieval system, or otherwise, without the prior written permission of the publisher.

Printed in the United States of America
07/08

Copyright© American Book Company. DO NOT DUPLICATE. 1-888-264-5877.

Copyright© American Book Company. DO NOT DUPLICATE. 1-888-264-5877.

# ACT Reading Test Preparation Guide
# Preface

The *ACT® Reading Test Preparation Guide* will help students preparing to take the ACT Reading Test. The most up-to-date requirements and strategies for the ACT Reading Test are covered in this book. The materials presented here will also help students who want to retake the ACT Reading Test to improve their previous score. ACT® is a registered trademark of ACT, Inc. American Book Company is not affiliated with ACT, Inc., and produced this book independently.

This book contains several sections: 1) general information about the book, 2) a complete diagnostic reading test, 3) an evaluation chart, 4) chapters that review the strategies, concepts, and skills that improve readiness for the ACT Reading Test, and 5) two complete practice reading tests. Answers to the practice tests, chapter practices, and chapter reviews are in a separate manual.

We welcome your comments and suggestions. Please contact us at

**American Book Company**

**PO Box 2638**

**Woodstock, GA 30188-1383**

**Toll Free: 1 (888) 264-5877**

**Phone: (770) 928-2834**

**Fax: 1 (866) 827-3240**

**Web site: www.americanbookcompany.com**

Copyright © American Book Company. DO NOT DUPLICATE. 1-888-264-5877.

# ABOUT THE AUTHORS

**Rob Hunter** is Copy Editor and ELA Writer at American Book Company. He has more than ten years of experience teaching grammar, reading, English composition, and other subjects to students at various levels. He graduated from Georgia State University in 1995 with a Bachelor of Arts in English.

**Jason Kirk**, Copy Editor and ELA Writer at American Book Company, graduated from Kennesaw State University with a bachelor's degree in English. In addition to writing short fiction and political opinion, he has worked in middle and high schools and tutored college writers.

**About the Project Coordinator: Zuzana Urbanek** serves as ELA Curriculum Coordinator for American Book Company. She is a professional writer with twenty-five years of experience in education, business, and publishing. She has taught a variety of English courses since 1990 at the college level and also taught English as a foreign language abroad. Her master's degree is from Arizona State University.

**About the Executive Editor: Dr. Frank J. Pintozzi** is a former Professor of Education at Kennesaw State University. For over twenty-eight years, he has taught English and reading at the high school and college levels as well as in teacher preparation courses in language arts and social studies. In addition to writing and editing state standard-specific texts for high school exit and end of course exams, he has edited and written numerous college textbooks.

Copyright © American Book Company. DO NOT DUPLICATE. 1-888-264-5877.

# ACT Reading
# Diagnostic Test

35 Minutes—40 Questions

**DIRECTIONS:** There are four passages in this test. Each passage is followed by ten questions. After reading a passage, choose the best answer to each question. You may refer to the passages as often as necessary.

Copyright © American Book Company. DO NOT DUPLICATE. 1-888-264-5877.

## Passage I

**PROSE FICTION:** This passage is adapted from *Babbitt* by Sinclair Lewis.

1   The Good Citizens' League had spread through the country, but nowhere was it so effective and well esteemed as in cities of the type of
5   Zenith, commercial cities of a few hundred thousand inhabitants, most of which—though not all—lay inland, against a background of cornfields and mines and of small towns which
10   depended upon them for mortgage-loans, table-manners, art, social philosophy and millinery.

   To the League belonged most of the prosperous citizens of Zenith. They
15   were not all of the kind who called themselves "Regular Guys." Besides these hearty fellows, these salesmen of prosperity, there were the aristocrats, that is, the men who were richer or had
20   been rich for more generations: the presidents of banks and of factories, the land-owners, the corporation lawyers, the fashionable doctors, and the few young-old men who worked not at all
25   but, reluctantly remaining in Zenith, collected luster-ware and first editions as though they were back in Paris. All of them agreed that the working-classes must be kept in their place; and all of
30   them perceived that American Democracy did not imply any equality of wealth, but did demand a wholesome sameness of thought, dress, painting, morals, and vocabulary.

35   In this they were like the ruling-class of any other country, particularly of Great Britain, but they differed in being more vigorous and in actually trying to produce the accepted
40   standards which all classes, everywhere, desire, but usually despair of realizing.

   The longest struggle of the Good Citizens' League was against the Open
45   Shop—which was secretly a struggle against all union labor. Accompanying it was an Americanization Movement, with evening classes in English and history and economics, and daily
50   articles in the newspapers, so that newly arrived foreigners might learn that the true-blue and one hundred per cent American way of settling labor-troubles was for workmen to trust and
55   love their employers.

   The League was more than generous in approving other organizations which agreed with its aims. It helped the Y.M.C.A. to raise a
60   two-hundred-thousand-dollar fund for a new building. Babbitt, Vergil Gunch, Sidney Finkelstein, and even Charles McKelvey told the spectators at movie theaters how great an influence for
65   manly Christianity the "good old Y" had been in their own lives; and the hoar and mighty Colonel Rutherford Snow, owner of the *Advocate-Times,* was photographed clasping the hand of
70   Sheldon Smeeth of the Y.M.C.A. It is true that afterward, when Smeeth lisped, "You must come to one of our prayer-meetings," the ferocious Colonel bellowed, "What the hell
75   would I do that for? I've got a bar of my own," but this did not appear in the public prints.

   The League was of value to the American Legion at a time when
80   certain of the lesser and looser newspapers were criticizing that organization of veterans of the Great War. One evening a number of young men raided the Zenith Socialist

Copyright © American Book Company. DO NOT DUPLICATE. 1-888-264-5877.

85 Headquarters, burned its records, beat the office staff, and agreeably dumped desks out of the window. All of the newspapers save the *Advocate-Times* and the *Evening Advocate* attributed

90 this valuable but perhaps hasty direct-action to the American Legion. Then a flying squadron from the Good Citizens' League called on the unfair papers and explained that no ex-soldier

95 could possibly do such a thing, and the editors saw the light, and retained their advertising. When Zenith's lone Conscientious Objector came home from prison and was righteously run

100 out of town, the newspapers referred to the perpetrators as an "unidentified mob."

In all the activities and triumphs of the Good Citizens' League Babbitt

105 took part, and completely won back to self-respect, placidity, and the affection of his friends. But he began to protest, "Gosh, I've done my share in cleaning up the city. I want to tend to business.

110 Think I'll just kind of slacken up on this G.C.L. stuff now."

He had returned to the church as he had returned to the Boosters' Club. He had even endured the lavish greeting

115 which Sheldon Smeeth gave him. He was worried lest during his late discontent he had imperiled his salvation. He was not quite sure there was a Heaven to be attained, but Dr.

120 John Jennison Drew said there was, and Babbitt was not going to take a chance.

1. **The author states in lines 86–87 that a number of young men "agreeably dumped desks out of the window." The word *agreeably*, as it is used here, most likely means that the young men acted:**

   A. mildly.

   B. affably.

   C. enthusiastically.

   D. obligatorily.

2. **The main point of the second paragraph (lines 13–34) is that:**

   F. American Democracy does not imply any equality of wealth.

   G. The Good Citizens' League is controlled by Zenith's citizens that are well-to-do.

   H. The Good Citizens' League is not just made up of "Regular Guys."

   J. All who belong to the Good Citizens' League agree that the working-classes must be kept in their place.

3. **Considering the context in which it is found, the phrase "the editors saw the light" (lines 95–96) most likely means:**

   A. that the editors realized that they had reported something that they were not sure had really happened.

   B. that the editors had an experience of religious conversion.

   C. that the editors realized that the flying squadron from the Good Citizens' League was responsible for raiding the Zenith Socialist Headquarters.

   D. that the editors were pressured into acting with the interests of the Good Citizens' League in mind.

Copyright © American Book Company. DO NOT DUPLICATE. 1-888-264-5877.

4. **Based on information given in the passage, what would most likely be the reason that the *Advocate-Times* did NOT attribute the raid on the Socialist Headquarters to the American Legion?**

   F. The newspaper was unaware of the event.

   G. The newspaper did not consider such a story important.

   H. The newspaper did not want to give the American Legion press coverage.

   J. The newspaper has close connections to the American Legion.

5. **Based on details in the passage, Sheldon Smeeth would best be described as:**

   A. a practicing Christian.

   B. a soldier formerly under the command of Colonel Rutherford.

   C. an aristocrat.

   D. a "Regular Guy."

6. **Based on the passage, the Good Citizens' League could be described as an organization that:**

   I. is very influential in Zenith.

   II. supports labor unions.

   III. protects conscientious objectors.

   F. I only

   G. I and II only

   H. I and III only

   J. I, II, and III

7. **The author's attitude toward the Good Citizens' League in this passage would be best described as:**

   A. serious.

   B. appreciative.

   C. amused.

   D. sentimental.

8. **According to the information given in the passage, it can be inferred that the main difference between the Y.M.C.A. and the Zenith Socialists is what?**

   F. The Y.M.C.A. is made up of Christian members; the Zenith Socialists are not.

   G. The Y.M.C.A. does not have its headquarters in Zenith.

   H. The Zenith Socialists are supported by the *Evening Advocate* and the Y.M.C.A. is supported by the *Advocate-Times*.

   J. The Y.M.C.A. agrees with the aims of the Good Citizens' League; the Zenith Socialists do not.

9. **Based on the last two paragraphs (lines 103–121), what would best describe Babbitt's feelings about conformity?**

   A. He rejects it.

   B. He reluctantly accepts it.

   C. He embraces it.

   D. He has no choice; he must conform.

Copyright © American Book Company. DO NOT DUPLICATE. 1-888-264-5877.

**10. What effect(s) does the Good Citizens' League have on Zenith?**

    I. It strengthens the ruling class.

    II. It helps to maintain several important organizations.

    III. It encourages working class people to cooperate with their employers.

    **F.** I only

    **G.** III only

    **H.** I and II

    **J.** I, II, and III

### Passage II

**SOCIAL SCIENCE:** This passage is adapted from "Dogs of Summer" (©2008 American Book Company).

1     The typical American's culinary delight, the hot dog, has been around for so long that people now generally take it for granted. What is for many
5   people a staple of summer ballpark and picnic eating is actually about 400 years old as a Western food item. The early forerunner of the hot dog, the frankfurter (a type of sausage), most
10  likely originated in Germany. From there, it was carried over to the United States with the nineteenth-century wave of immigrants.

    This first version of the hot dog,
15  the frankfurter, has its own murky past. The sausage which became known as the frankfurter was created somewhere in Germany in either 1487 or the late 1600s, depending on whose story is
20  correct. The exact location is also disputed. The city of Frankfurt, which was first associated with the sausage, claims to be the place where it began in 1487. Here the sausage was nicknamed
25  *dachshund*, after the long-bodied

German hunting dog (*dachs*—badger + *hund*—hound). However, some food historians believe that a butcher from Coburg, Germany, invented the
30  sausage two centuries later and then took it to Frankfurt as a form of promotion. The name association between the food item and the city of Frankfurt would become a powerful
35  image in Germany.

    Once the frankfurter came to the United States, the story of how it morphed into the modern hot dog is likewise disputed. The most accepted
40  story is that a German immigrant began to sell "dachshunds" with milk rolls (small round rolls which did not cover the sausage ends) and sauerkraut (cooked cabbage and spice) from a
45  push cart. This was done in the Bowery section of New York City in the 1860s. In 1871, a German butcher opened the first Coney Island hot dog stand, wrapping the dachshund sausages in
50  the same type of rolls. The German food was embraced in Chicago in 1893 at the Colombian Exposition. Here, many tourists found the concoction of meat and bread to be a quick, tasty way
55  to have a warm meal while strolling through the exposition.

    But it was the connection with baseball that raised the American hot dog to new heights in tradition. The
60  owner of the St. Louis Browns, Chris Von der Ahe, himself a German immigrant and tavern owner, began (also in 1893) serving sausages at ball games. Other ballparks took up this
65  simple way to serve food in a convenient form.

Copyright © American Book Company. DO NOT DUPLICATE. 1-888-264-5877.

Some believe that not only the food item but the term *hot dog* itself is also associated with baseball. In 1901, sausage vendors at the New York Polo Grounds baseball stadium were serving food on a chilly April day. As they pulled heated sausages from hot water tanks, they were heard shouting, "They're red hot!" While the product was still referred to as dachshunds, a local sports cartoonist allegedly decided to mark the occasion by drawing a cartoon, showing barking dogs wrapped in buns, with heads, paws, and tails sticking out. His caption read "hot dog" because he did not know how to spell dachshund. The problem with this story, however, is that historians have not been able to locate any version of this cartoon, even though the artist worked for a major newspaper.

The American version of the hot dog bun was widely popularized in St. Louis in 1904, during the Louisiana Purchase Exposition. Expositions were considered national events and were well-attended by people from across the country. It was in this setting that Bavarian concessionaire Anton Feuchtwanger first tried to find a way to mollify the effect of the heated sausages on bare hands. At first, he gave away white gloves with the promise of their return. But when he ran out of gloves, he sought another way to keep hands from being scalded. His brother-in-law, a baker, then came up with an improvised roll. This new roll was a long, slender one that would fit the entire sausage, saving the hands of customers. People from around the country took this innovative idea home and so spread an enduring American tradition.

For most Americans, what we call a hot dog today was called a frank (short for frankfurter) until World War I, when anti-German feelings supposedly led to the more modern, colloquial term. After the war, the original, Germanic name regained its common usage. Franks are sold in grocery stores today—but when sold in-bun, the term hot dog is the name of choice—ketchup, mustard, and relish are all optional.

**11. As it is used in line 15, the phrase *murky past* most likely means:**

A. a dark past.

B. an obscure past.

C. a gloomy past.

D. a dreary past.

**12. The main point of the fifth paragraph (lines 67–88) is that:**

F. the term "hot dog" may have been created by a sports cartoonist.

G. hot dogs were named as such because they were hot.

H. no one really knows for sure where the term "hot dog" came from.

J. hot dogs got their name from dachshunds, or wiener dogs.

**13. According to the passage, the hot dog most likely appeared in the United States:**

A. in the 1600s.

B. in the 1700s.

C. in the 1800s.

D. in the 1900s.

Copyright © American Book Company. DO NOT DUPLICATE. 1-888-264-5877.

14. **According to one story in the passage, the hot dog became associated with baseball after:**

    F. the New York Yankees won the first World Series.

    G. sausage vendors sold them at Coney Island in 1871.

    H. the words "hot dog" were written in a caption under the drawing of a barking dog wrapped in a bun.

    J. World War I.

15. **According to the passage, if you were to buy a hot dog in St. Louis in 1904, how would it likely have been served to you?**

    I. with milk rolls which did not cover the sausage ends

    II. with white gloves to mollify the effect of the heated sausage on the hands

    III. with a long, slender roll that fit the entire sausage

    A. I only

    B. II only

    C. III only

    D. II and III only

16. **We can infer from the passage that the hot dogs that were sold at the New York Polo Grounds in 1901 were served:**

    I. with milk rolls which did not cover the sausage ends

    II. with white gloves to mollify the effect of the heated sausage on the hands

    III. with a long, slender roll that fit the entire sausage

    F. I only

    G. II only

    H. III only

    J. II and III only

17. **According to the passage, the term "hot dog" borrows from the word:**

    A. Frankfurt.

    B. dachshund.

    C. Germany.

    D. sausage.

18. **According to the passage, the term *frank*:**

    I. was used by most Americans to describe the popular sausage until World War I.

    II. is short for frankfurter.

    III. was replaced by most Americans with the term *hot dog* because of anti-German feelings.

    F. I only

    G. II only

    H. II and III only

    J. I, II, and III

Copyright © American Book Company. DO NOT DUPLICATE. 1-888-264-5877.

**19. According to the passage, which of the following is NOT true about the hot dog?**

A. Its roots begin in Germany.

B. The facts of its history are not completely agreed upon.

C. It was not introduced to the United States for its first 200–300 years.

D. Its popularity suffered greatly during World War I.

**20. As it is used in line 98, the word *mollify* most likely means:**

F. to cool down.

G. to soothe.

H. to sweeten.

J. to mellow.

## Passage III

**HUMANITIES:** This passage is adapted from *The Poetry of Architecture* by John Ruskin.

1    We advanced a position in the last paper, that silence is never perfect without motion. That is, unless something which might possibly
5    produce sound is evident to the eye, the absence of sound is not surprising to the ear, and, therefore, not impressive. Let it be observed, for instance, how much the stillness of a summer's
10    evening is enhanced by the perception of the gliding and majestic motion of some calm river, strong but still; or of the high and purple clouds; or of the voiceless leaves, among the opening
15    branches. To produce this impression, however, the motion must be uniform, though not necessarily slow. One of the chief peculiarities of the ocean thoroughfares of Venice, is the
20    remarkable silence which rests upon them, enhanced as it is by the swift, but beautifully uniform, motion of the gondola. Now, there is no motion more uniform, silent or beautiful than that of
25    smoke; and, therefore, when we wish the peace or stillness of a scene to be impressive, it is highly useful to draw the attention to it.

In the cottage, therefore, a building
30    peculiarly adapted for scenes of peace, the chimney, as conducting the eye to what is agreeable, may be considered as important, and, if well managed, a beautiful accompaniment. But in
35    buildings of a higher class, smoke ceases to be interesting. Owing to their general greater elevation, it is relieved against the sky, instead of against a dark background, thereby losing the
40    fine silvery blue,—which among trees,

Copyright © American Book Company. DO NOT DUPLICATE. 1-888-264-5877.

or rising out of a distant country, is so exquisitely beautiful,—and assuming a dingy yellowish black: its motion becomes useless; for the idea of
45 stillness is no longer desirable, or, at least, no longer attainable, being interrupted by the nature of the building itself: and, finally, the associations it arouses are not
50 dignified; we may think of a comfortable fireside, perhaps, but are quite as likely to dream of kitchens, and spits, and shoulders of mutton. None of these imaginations are in their place, if
55 the character of the building be elevated; they are barely tolerable in the dwelling house and the street. Now, when smoke is objectionable, it is certainly improper to direct attention to
60 the chimney; and, therefore, for two weighty reasons, decorated chimneys, of any sort or size whatsoever, are inexcusable barbarisms; first, because, where smoke is beautiful, decoration is
65 unsuited to the building; and secondly, because, where smoke is ugly, decoration directs attention to its ugliness.

It is unfortunately a prevailing idea
70 with some of our architects, that what is a disagreeable object in itself may be relieved or concealed by lavish ornament; and there never was a greater mistake. It should be a general
75 principle, that what is intrinsically ugly should be utterly destitute of ornament, that the eye may not be drawn to it. The pretended skulls of the three Magi at Cologne are set in gold, and have a
80 diamond in each eye; and are a thousand times more ghastly than if their brown bones had been left in peace. Such an error as this ought never to be committed in architecture. If any

85 part of the building has disagreeable associations connected with it, let it alone: do not ornament it. Keep it subdued, and simply adapted to its use; and the eye will not go to it, nor quarrel
90 with it. It would have been well if this principle had been kept in view in the renewal of some of the public buildings in Oxford. In All Souls College, for instance, the architect has carried his
95 chimneys half as high as all the rest of the building, and fretted them with Gothic. The eye is instantly caught by the plated candlestick-like columns, and runs with some complacency up
100 the groining and fret-work, and alights finally and fatally on a red chimney-top. He might as well have built a Gothic aisle at an entrance to a coal wharf. We have no scruple in saying
105 that the man who could desecrate the Gothic trefoil into an ornament for a chimney has not the slightest feeling, and never will have any, of its beauty or its use; he was never born to be an
110 architect, and never will be one.

**21. As it is used in line 37, the word *relieved* most nearly means:**

A. alleviated.

B. freed from distress.

C. made prominent.

D. made less unpleasant.

Copyright © American Book Company. DO NOT DUPLICATE. 1-888-264-5877.

22. **What is the main point of the third paragraph (lines 69–110)?**

    F. If something looks ugly, do not draw attention to it.

    G. If something looks ugly, try to draw attention away from it.

    H. If something looks ugly, cover it up with something better.

    J. If something looks ugly, try to decorate it.

23. **According to the first paragraph, the absence of sound is "impressive" when:**

    A. one visits Venice.

    B. one enjoys a summer's evening.

    C. one is observing smoke.

    D. one would expect sound from something in motion.

24. **Based on the details in the third paragraph, if people at All Souls College were to find themselves looking at the smoke coming from the tops of buildings, what most likely drew their attention there?**

    F. the skulls of the three Magi, set in gold with a diamond in each eye

    G. a fire in the building

    H. a Gothic aisle at the entrance of the building

    J. Gothic style chimneys half as high as the rest of the building

25. **According to the author, what would NOT be a good reason to build a chimney?**

    I. to direct smoke out of the building

    II. to draw attention to smoke

    III. to decorate a building

    A. I only

    B. III only

    C. II and III

    D. I, II, and III

26. **According to the author, which of the following is NOT considered to be an appealing characteristic of smoke?**

    F. its motion

    G. its aroma

    H. its beauty

    J. its silence

27. **According to the author, the motion of smoke loses its appeal under all of the following conditions EXCEPT:**

    A. when the building is of a lower elevation.

    B. when smoke can no longer be seen against a dark background.

    C. when smoke makes a person think of kitchens, spits, and mutton.

    D. when the chimney is tall and attention-grabbing.

Copyright © American Book Company. DO NOT DUPLICATE. 1-888-264-5877.

28. **Which of the following is NOT a reason that the author finds the three Magi at Cologne (lines 77–83) to be "ghastly"?**

    F. The skulls are brown.

    G. The skulls are set in gold.

    H. The skulls have a diamond in each eye.

    J. The skulls draw attention to themselves.

29. **According to the third paragraph, how are the three Magi at Cologne and the chimneys at All Souls College similar?**

    A. They both draw attention to something ugly.

    B. They are both found in England.

    C. They are both decorated in elaborate Gothic style.

    D. They both feature excessive gold and diamonds.

30. **Based on the passage, what would best describe the author's attitude toward his subject?**

    F. narrow-minded

    G. adamant

    H. pessimistic

    J. reserved

Copyright © American Book Company. DO NOT DUPLICATE. 1-888-264-5877.

**Passage IV**

**NATURAL SCIENCE:** This passage is adapted from "On the Edge of Vertigo" (©2008 American Book Company).

1   In U2's 2004 hit single "Vertigo," earnest frontman Bono sings, "I'm at a place called vertigo / it's everything I wish I didn't know." The opening verse
5   suggests a powerless person, trapped and bewildered as "lights go down," traveling through "the jungle is your head." The song is about how a loving relationship can provide stability in
10  confusing and turbulent times, but much of the imagery describes a desperate kind of confused despair.

    These parts of the song's lyrics paint a stylized picture of vertigo, the
15  actual medical condition, which is an extremely uncomfortable state of dizziness that causes a person to sense that his or her surroundings are whirling in a vortex of preternatural
20  shapes and colors. A person in the grip of severe vertigo can do little more than lie prone, as merely raising up to look around can be an impossible task. Even in mild cases, sensations of dizziness
25  and loss of control can produce panic. There are several causes of vertigo, usually associated with a disorder of the inner ear (vestibular labyrinth), where center of balance is maintained.
30  Even an ear infection can bring about mild vertigo. But there are more serious conditions that lead to a type of vertigo that is often unbearable.

    One of the worst of these occurs to
35  people who are afflicted by Meniere's disease. Meniere's has several unsettling symptoms, but vertigo may be the worst. The condition, named after nineteenth-century French doctor
40  Prosper Meniere, begins with increased

fluid pressure in the inner ear. The disease is typified by sudden, and occasionally severe, vertigo. Some people suffer a mild form with only a
45 brief and temporary rush of dizziness. However, others have to deal with infrequent episodes that, while somewhat manageable, can cause anxiety and dread and may grievously
50 affect quality of life.

The disease is not life-threatening, but it is debilitating. A person suffering from the severe form of Meniere's experiences sudden bouts of vertigo
55 that cause nausea and vomiting. The average attack lasts two to four hours, and may end with a very calm, sedated stage. After the most severe attacks, people are exhausted and can recover
60 only if able to sleep for several hours. However, when dizziness returns, the process begins all over again. One major problem is that there are no clear warning signals for a person with this
65 disease. It may strike at any time and any place. Sometimes the victim will feel "fullness" in the ear, but that is not much of a reliable indicator.

The tools for living with the disease
70 range from monitoring the diet to taking medications to having surgery. People with Meniere's should eat little salt and avoid caffeine. Drugs can alleviate certain symptoms:
75 prescription drugs like meclizine control the dizzying vertigo effects; promethazine or prochlorperazine are meant to handle nausea; and trazodone helps relieve anxiety. An antibiotic is
80 sometimes injected into the inner ear, where it is absorbed; the injection dulls the balancing mechanism of the afflicted ear, so that the other ear takes over in controlling balance. This rest

85 gives the medicated ear a chance to heal or at least take a break. Most cases of Meniere's begin with only one ear, but usually the other ear becomes affected as well.

90 Operations are attempted only in the severest cases—when nothing else seems to be helping. Genetics seem to play a role in the severity of the vertigo and its resistance to treatment. A
95 labyrinthectomy, or removal of the inner ear, can be used if deafness has already occurred anyway. Another surgery, a vestibular neurectomy, neutralizes the inner ear by cutting the
100 nerve that controls balance, thus relegating the task of balance to the healthy ear.

Why this disease develops is still unclear to doctors, but most often it
105 strikes those who have had prior ear trouble—such as chronic infections, injury, or other issues affecting the ear canal. Uncertainty about the causes of the disease is perhaps almost as
110 disturbing to sufferers as the physical damage itself. Bono may not be much of a medical expert, but his line, "the night is full of holes," may suggest how the bleakness of vertigo is only
115 exacerbated by what we do not know about the condition.

31. **As it is used in line 19, the word *preternatural* most nearly means:**

   A. beautiful.

   B. supernatural.

   C. extraordinary.

   D. miraculous.

Copyright © American Book Company. DO NOT DUPLICATE. 1-888-264-5877.

**32.** The main point of the fifth paragraph (lines 69–89) is that:

  **F.** there are several tools for managing Meniere's disease.

  **G.** usually, both ears are affected by Meniere's disease.

  **H.** injecting antibiotics into the inner ear is the most effective way to treat Meniere's disease.

  **J.** prescription drugs alleviate different symptoms of Meniere's disease.

**33.** As it is used in line 101, the word *relegating* most nearly means:

  **A.** banishing.

  **B.** classifying.

  **C.** downgrading.

  **D.** transferring.

**34.** According to the passage, after a severe attack of vertigo, a victim will likely experience all of the following EXCEPT:

  **F.** a need to sleep for several hours.

  **G.** a calming stage.

  **H.** a "fullness" in the ear.

  **J.** a feeling of exhaustion.

**35.** Meniere's disease is named after:

  **A.** Bono, the lead singer of the group U2.

  **B.** famous jeweler Paul-Nicolas Meniere, who had the disease.

  **C.** Prosper Meniere, a French doctor in the 1800s.

  **D.** the French word for dizzy.

**36.** Based on information presented in the fifth paragraph (lines 69–89), a vertigo sufferer successfully treated with the prescription drugs meclizine and promethazine may still experience which of the following symptoms?

  **F.** anxiety

  **G.** nausea

  **H.** vertigo

  **J.** dizziness

**37.** To what does the author compare the "holes" in the U2 music lyrics in the last paragraph (line 113)?

  I. chronic infections, injury, or other issues affecting the ear canal

  II. uncertainty about the causes of Meniere's Disease

  III. the physical and emotional damage caused by Meniere's Disease

  **A.** I only

  **B.** II only

  **C.** II and III only

  **D.** I, II, and III

**38.** According to the passage, which of the following is NOT one of the possible effects of Meniere's Disease?

  **F.** severe vertigo

  **G.** nausea

  **H.** anxiety

  **J.** headaches

Copyright © American Book Company. DO NOT DUPLICATE. 1-888-264-5877.

**39.** Based on information in the passage, if a person has been diagnosed with Meniere's Disease and has been ordered by a doctor to alter his or her diet, which of the following should he or she avoid?

A. carrots

B. coffee

C. aspirin

D. alcohol

**40.** According to the passage, Meniere's Disease:

F. can be life-threatening, if sufferers do not rest.

G. begins with increased fluid pressure in the ear.

H. will never cause deafness.

J. is a dizzying symptom of vertigo.

# ACT READING DIAGNOSTIC TEST EVALUATION CHART

On the following chart, circle the question numbers that you answered incorrectly, and evaluate the results. Then turn to the appropriate topics (listed by chapters), read the explanations, and complete the exercises. Review the other chapters as needed. Finally, complete the practice tests at the end of this book to further prepare yourself for the ACT Reading Test.

NOTE: Some questions may appear under multiple chapters, because those questions require multiple skills.

| Chapter Number | Question Number |
|---|---|
| Chapter 2: Reading for Understanding | 1, 2, 3, 6, 11, 12, 13, 14, 20, 21, 22, 23, 24, 31, 32, 33, 34, 35 |
| Chapter 3: Critical Reading | 4, 5, 7, 8, 9, 10, 15, 16, 17, 18, 19, 25, 26, 27, 28, 29, 30, 36, 37, 38, 39, 40 |
| Chapter 4: Interpreting Prose Fiction Texts | 1–10 |
| Chapter 5: Interpreting Humanities Texts | 21–30 |
| Chapter 6: Interpreting Social Studies Texts | 11–20 |
| Chapter 7: Interpreting Natural Sciences Texts | 31–40 |

Copyright © American Book Company. DO NOT DUPLICATE. 1-888-264-5877.

# Chapter 1
# Preparing for the ACT Reading Test

## THE ACT READING TEST

This book focuses on the **Reading Test** portion of the ACT. When you take the ACT, you will be given thirty-five minutes to answer forty questions in the Reading section.

The Reading Test is designed to measure your skills in reading. Questions are based on four types of reading selections: prose fiction, humanities, social studies, and natural sciences. Each of these four selections is followed by ten questions that measure your reading comprehension, so each section counts for 25 percent of the overall score.

**Prose fiction** questions are based on a short story or an excerpt from a story or novel.

**Humanities** questions are based on an excerpt from a memoir or personal essay or on a passage in the content area of architecture, art, dance, ethics, film, language, literary criticism, music, philosophy, radio, television, or theater.

**Social studies** questions are based on a passage in the content area of anthropology, archaeology, biography, business, economics, education, geography, history, political science, psychology, or sociology.

**Natural sciences** questions are based on a passage in the content area of anatomy, astronomy, biology, botany, chemistry, ecology, geology, medicine, meteorology, microbiology, natural history, physiology, physics, technology, or zoology.

Two subscores also are given. The social studies/sciences subscore is based on the questions in the social studies and the natural sciences sections of the test, and the arts/literature subscore is based on the questions in the prose fiction and humanities sections of the test.

You do not need to be knowledgeable about science, social studies, literature, or any other topic to succeed on the test. However, you do need to read carefully and think about what you are reading. Remember, the ACT Reading Test is measuring your skills in reading and understanding.

Copyright © American Book Company. DO NOT DUPLICATE. 1-888-264-5877.

# TYPES OF QUESTIONS

You will see two types of questions on the Reading Test.

**Referring** questions ask you to find or use information that is clearly stated in the passage.

**Reasoning** questions ask you to take information that's either stated or implied and use it to answer more complex questions.

Most questions ask you to:

- identify or interpret details
- determine the main idea of a paragraph, a section, or a passage
- understand comparative relationships (comparisons and contrasts)
- understand cause-effect relationships
- make generalizations
- determine the meanings of words from context
- understand sequences of events
- draw conclusions about the author's voice and method

The diagnostic test at the beginning and two practice tests at the end of this book are simulated ACT tests. They are the same length and contain passages and questions comparable to those you will see on the ACT. Review your scores on these tests with your teacher or tutor to determine if there are skill areas you need to hone before taking the ACT.

For practice with other sections of the ACT, refer to these titles from American Book Company:

*ACT English Test Preparation Guide*

*ACT Mathematics Test Preparation Guide*

*ACT Science Test Preparation Guide*

# FREQUENTLY ASKED QUESTIONS

## WHAT IS THE ACT?

The ACT is a national college admission examination which is accepted by virtually all US colleges and universities. The exam measures the knowledge, understanding, and skills that you have gained throughout your education.

## HOW LONG IS THE EXAM?

The full ACT includes 215 multiple-choice questions and takes approximately three hours and thirty minutes to complete (just over four hours if you are taking the optional Writing Test). Actual testing time is two hours and fifty-five minutes (plus thirty minutes if you are taking the Writing Test). The exam has four sections: English, math, reading, and science.

Copyright © American Book Company. DO NOT DUPLICATE. 1-888-264-5877.

## WHEN DO I TAKE THE ACT?

The ACT is administered in October, December, February, April, and June (in some states, it is also offered in September). When you take the ACT will depend on both when you feel ready and when you need test scores to include with applications to colleges.

## IS THERE A FEE?

Yes. The basic registration fee (currently $30.00 for the basic test or $44.50 if also taking the Writing Test) includes score reports for up to four colleges for which a valid code is listed at the time that you register. If you can't afford the registration fee, you may be eligible for an ACT Fee Waiver. For more information, see your high school guidance office.

For more details about the ACT, please visit ACT, Inc., at www.actstudent.org.

## TIPS FOR ACT PREPARATION AND TESTING

The ACT measures your overall learning, so if you have paid attention in school, you should do well! It would be difficult, if not impossible, to "cram" for an exam as comprehensive as this. However, you can study wisely by using an ACT-specific guide (like this book) and practice answering questions of the type that will be asked on the ACT (included in this book). Additional practice tests are available online from ACT, Inc., at www.actstudent.org/sampletest.

### PREPARING FOR THE ACT

- **Believe in yourself!** Attitude plays a big part in how well you do in anything. Keep your thoughts positive. Tell yourself you will do well on the exam.

- **Be prepared.** Get a good night's sleep the day before your exam. Eat a well-balanced meal, one that contains plenty of proteins and carbohydrates, prior to your exam.

- **Arrive early.** Allow yourself at least fifteen to twenty minutes to find your room and get settled. Then you can relax before the exam so you won't feel rushed.

- **Practice relaxation techniques.** Some students become overly worried about exams. Before or during the test, they may perspire heavily, experience an upset stomach, or have shortness of breath. If you feel any of these symptoms before the test, talk to a close friend or see a counselor for ways to deal with test anxiety. Here are some quick ways to relieve test anxiety:

  •**Imagine yourself in your favorite place.** Let yourself sit there and relax.

  •**Do a body scan.** Tense and relax each part of your body starting with your toes and ending with your forehead.

  •**Use the 3-12-6 method of relaxation** when you feel stress. Inhale slowly for three seconds. Hold your breath for twelve seconds, and then exhale slowly for six seconds.

Copyright © American Book Company. DO NOT DUPLICATE. 1-888-264-5877.

## TAKING THE ACT

- Carefully **read the instructions** on the ACT test booklet. You can read these instructions ahead of time at www.actstudent.org to make sure that you understand them.

- Once you are told that you may open the booklet, thoroughly **read the directions** for a test section before reading its corresponding passage or answering its questions.

- **Read each question carefully**, and use your best approach for answering the questions. Some test-takers like to skim the questions and answers before reading the passage. Others prefer to read the passage before looking at the questions. Decide which approach works best for you.

- **Answer each question** on the exam, as your score is based on the number of questions answered correctly. There is no penalty for guessing, but every spot left blank is automatically a zero.

- If you are uncertain about an answer, **take an educated guess**. Eliminate choices that are definitely wrong, and then choose from the remaining answers.

- **Use your answer sheet correctly**. Make sure the number on your question matches the number on your answer sheet. If you need to change your answer, erase it completely. Use a number two pencil, and make sure the answers are dark. The computerized scanner may skip over answers that are too light.

- **Check your answers**. If you finish a test before time is called, review your exam to make sure you have chosen the best responses. Change answers only if you are sure they are wrong.

- Be sure to **pace yourself**. Since you will have a limited amount of time, be careful not to spend too much time on one passage, leaving no time to complete the rest of the test. Listen for the announcement of five minutes remaining on each test.

- When time is called for each test, **put your pencil down**. If you continue to write or erase, you run the risk of being dismissed and your test being disqualified from scoring.

## WHAT TO LOOK FOR WHEN YOU TAKE THE READING TEST

- The Reading Test is comprised of **four essays** (or passages), one each focusing on prose fiction, humanities, social studies, and natural sciences.

- **Read the whole passage** quickly but carefully. Questions may ask you about parts of the passage and may refer to particular paragraphs, but ultimately they all reply on your understanding of the passage as a whole.

- Pay attention to the **advance organizers**, the brief title and explanation at the beginning of each passage. These brief intros tell the reader which area the passage is covering (prose fiction, humanities, social studies, and natural sciences), what the passage is about, and where it came from. It also may provide some additional information that will be helpful in understanding the passage.

Copyright © American Book Company. DO NOT DUPLICATE. 1-888-264-5877.

- Don't get tripped up by your existing knowledge about the topic of a passage. Remember that the Reading Test does not measure your subject-matter knowledge—it **assesses how well you *read***. There is a reason why many questions begin, "According to the passage…" or similarly. So, if you have an interest in architecture and see a humanities passage about it, be sure to read what it says rather than relying on previous knowledge; after all, the author's conclusions may not coincide with what you have learned in the past.

- **Read the answer choices carefully**. Although there are no "trick questions" on the ACT, there may be subtle differences in answers. If two answers seem to make sense to you, read them again, determine how they differ, and decide which one *best* answers the questions.

- There is always only **one correct answer** to each test question. However, some ACT test questions are followed by three Roman numerals containing information that might be used to compose the single correct answer. The information following only one Roman numeral might be the correct answer. The information following two of the Roman numerals might be the correct answer. Or the information following all three Roman numerals might be the correct answer. For an example, look at question 8 on page 25.

# HOW THE ACT READING TEST WILL LOOK

On the ACT Reading Test, you may see any of a great variety of passages in four umbrella subject areas: **prose fiction**, **humanities**, **social studies**, and **natural sciences**. The passages in this book cannot represent every type of passage you will see, but they will provide practice for reading and for answering the types of questions you will see on the actual test.

No matter what the subject of the passage, you are likely to find some of each of the following types of questions about it:

**Details**—Some questions will ask about details to see whether you read and understood them. These questions may ask what is true or included in a passage; they also may ask you to find the one answer that is NOT supported by the information in a passage. Questions that contain words like "NOT" or "EXCEPT" are called reverse questions, and you may see this format in questions about details or concepts.

**Main ideas**—To answer these questions, focus on the main point of a paragraph or the passage as a whole. Some questions may ask about "one of the main ideas" of a paragraph or passage, and this wording makes it important to rule out choices that are either supporting ideas or misstatements of what the passage says. For prose fiction and humanities passages, questions may ask about a main conflict or main theme, rather than a main idea.

**Comparative relationships**—These questions ask you to identify or interpret similarities or differences between ideas, events, characters, and so on. Some are straightforward questions about comparisons and contrasts presented in a passage, while others require you to perceive subtle similarities and differences.

**Cause-effect relationships**—Some questions may ask about the causes of an event or about the effects of something happening. For prose fiction, this can relate to how characters behave, and in nonfiction passages, it may refer to processes or history.

Copyright © American Book Company. DO NOT DUPLICATE. 1-888-264-5877.

**Generalizations**—These questions ask you to look concisely at what you read and make a general observation. Questions may ask you to conclude something or to make an inference about an event, idea, or character.

**Meanings of words**—For some questions, you will need to determine the meaning of words or phrases in context.

**Sequence of events**—These questions, sometimes tied to cause-effect relationships, ask that you relate when events happened in the sequence of a passage.

**Author's voice and method**—Some questions may ask about the author's style, attitude, and point of view or about the purpose for writing.

Read the following excerpt from a passage, try answering the questions that follow on your own, and then study the explanations about which answer is the correct one and why.

### Excerpt from a Sample Passage

**NATURAL SCIENCE:** This passage is adapted from an essay called "The Importance of Trees in Cities" by Leah Hallman Ott (©2007 American Book Company).

1    Heat from the earth is held in our atmosphere by carbon dioxide ($CO_2$) and other heat-trapping gases that prohibit it from releasing into space.
5    When high levels of these gases accumulate and trap excess heat, this phenomenon is known as the "greenhouse effect." Trees remove the $CO_2$ from the atmosphere during
10    photosynthesis, which forms carbohydrates that are used in plant structure, and return oxygen back to the atmosphere as a byproduct. Nearly half of the greenhouse effect is caused by
15    $CO_2$. Trees actually act as a carbon sink by removing the carbon and storing it in their trunks, branches, leaves, and roots while releasing oxygen back into the air.

        Trees also reduce the greenhouse
20    effect by shading our homes and office buildings. The shade that trees produce reduces our need for air conditioning by 30%, which reduces the amount of fossil fuels burned to produce
25    electricity. The combination of $CO_2$ removal from the atmosphere, carbon storage in wood, and the cooling effect of shade make trees a very efficient tool for fighting the greenhouse effect. In
30    fact, one tree that shades a home in the city will not only save fossil fuel, but it also will cut the $CO_2$ buildup as much as fifteen forest trees. It is estimated that a single mature tree in the city can absorb
35    carbon dioxide at a rate of forty-eight pounds per year and release enough oxygen back into our atmosphere to support two human beings. If every American family planted just one tree,
40    the amount of $CO_2$ in the atmosphere would be reduced by one billion pounds annually. This is almost 5 percent of the amount that such human activity as burning of fossil fuels pumps into the
45    atmosphere each year. So it is easy to see that the simple act of planting trees remains one of the cheapest, most effective means of drawing excess $CO_2$ from our atmosphere.

Copyright © American Book Company. DO NOT DUPLICATE. 1-888-264-5877.

## Sample Questions and Explanations

First, the "advance organizer" above the passage gives you several helpful details. It signifies that this is an excerpt from a Natural Science passage. It also provides the title of the original essay, which tells you that the passage as a whole is about the benefits of trees in an urban environment. These are important clues!

Now, try answering the following questions about the passage excerpt.

1. **Which of the following questions is NOT answered by the information in the passage?**
   A. How many trees does it take to annually remove forty-eight pounds of $CO_2$ from the atmosphere?
   B. What gases act to trap heat in the earth's atmosphere and prevent them from being released into space?
   C. During photosynthesis, what byproduct do trees return into the atmosphere?
   D. What would happen if every American planted just one tree?

Which answer did you choose? This is a **details** question that requires you to pay attention to the cause-effect relationships covered in the passage. **The best answer is B.** The first paragraph does talk about $CO_2$ being a gas that traps heat in the atmosphere, but the "other gases" that contribute are not mentioned. The question in **A** is answered in the second paragraph ("…a single mature tree in the city can absorb carbon dioxide at a rate of forty-eight pounds per year…"); **C** is answered in the first paragraph ("…during photosynthesis which forms carbohydrates that are used in plant structure and return oxygen back to the atmosphere as a byproduct"); **D** is answered in the second paragraph ("If every American family

planted just one tree, the amount of $CO_2$ in the atmosphere would be reduced by one billion pounds annually").

2. **The main point of this passage is that:**
   F. heat from the earth is held in the earth's atmosphere by carbon dioxide and other heat-trapping gases that prohibit it from releasing into space.
   G. the phenomenon known as the "greenhouse effect" occurs when high levels of gases accumulate and trap excess heat in the earth's atmosphere.
   H. trees reduce the greenhouse effect by removing $CO_2$ from the atmosphere and by providing shade for homes and buildings.
   J. planting trees is something that every American should do to help improve the environment.

Copyright © American Book Company. DO NOT DUPLICATE. 1-888-264-5877.

Clearly, this is a **main ideas** question. To answer it correctly, you need to have read the passage and understood its focus. When reading a full passage, don't rely on the main point being summed up in the first or last paragraph, and remember that every writer does not necessarily make the first sentence serve as the topic sentence. A good way to decide the focus of a passage is to think about how you would sum up what it says in one sentence. Clues can also come from the title of the passage. The idea that trees reduce the greenhouse effect and how they do this is the main focus of this passage. **The best answer is H.** Choices **F** and **G** are supporting details that describe the greenhouse effect, but they do not mention trees; **J** is an opinion that may be supported by the passage, but it is neither stated by the author, nor does it sum up the focus of the passage as a whole.

Copyright © American Book Company. DO NOT DUPLICATE. 1-888-264-5877.

3. **Which of the following statements would be most effective for the author to add to help support the ideas in the passage?**

   **A.** A recent warming of the earth's lower atmosphere, called "global warming," is believed to be due to increased concentrations of greenhouse gases in the atmosphere.

   **B.** Trees are an important element of the natural landscape because they help to prevent soil erosion and provide a sheltered ecosystem in and under their foliage.

   **C.** A study in the 1990s showed that part of the Maldives islands under a pollution cloud, blown south from India, had about a 10% reduction in sunlight reaching the surface.

   **D.** Deforestation and forest fires contribute to the greenhouse effect because, as the number of trees declines, less carbon dioxide can be recycled, and their burning releases more carbon.

This is a combination question about **author's voice and method** and **comparative relationships**. First, it requires that you determine the author's attitude from the information in the passage. Although the passage is predominantly factual, statements about human activity pumping greenhouse gases into the atmosphere and the cheap, effective results of planting trees do show that the author thinks it is a good idea to use trees to help the environment. Next, it asks you to compare this viewpoint with the statements offered in the answer choices and choose the one that best fits with the author's stance. Choice **A** extends the idea of greenhouse gases to global warming, which may sound like an appropriate point to add. But is it the most effective choice? **B** contains information about trees which is interesting but not relevant, and **C** is unrelated information about a different environmental issue. **The best answer is D**, which directly applies to the author's main point about the relationship between trees and the greenhouse effect.

Copyright © American Book Company. DO NOT DUPLICATE. 1-888-264-5877.

4. **In the first paragraph, when the author says that trees act as a *carbon sink*, this most likely means that:**

   F. trees are a source of carbon dioxide.

   G. trees funnel away $CO_2$, helping to clean the air.

   H. trees use carbon dioxide as fuel during photosynthesis.

   J. trees in low-lying areas are best at converting $CO_2$ to oxygen.

This is a question about the **meanings of words**. In this case, you need to identify the term *carbon sink*. You may recall the term from science classes, but even if you do not, you can decipher its meaning from the context of the passage. Everything in the passage points away from **F** being the right answer; the passage talks about trees removing $CO_2$ from the atmosphere. **The best answer is G** because it describes what trees do and relates it to the term "sink" through vocabulary like "funnel away" and "clean." Choice **H** is a true statement, but there is nothing to indicate how this relates to the term "carbon sink." Finally, **J** is an unsupported, illogical statement.

5. **A reasonable conclusion that you can draw from the passage is that:**

   A. planting trees around your home can reduce your electric bill.

   B. one tree should be planted for every city block to reduce $CO_2$.

   C. it is easier to breathe in a lush forest than in an urban center.

   D. deciduous trees are the most important plant life on the planet.

This **generalizations** question asks you decide which answer choice is supported by facts in the passage. **The best answer is A**; the second paragraph says, "The shade that trees produce reduces our need for air conditioning by 30%, which reduces the amount of fossil fuels burned to produce electricity." While **B** and **C** may seem like reasonable conclusions, neither one is supported by information in the passage. Choice **D** is an unsupported opinion.

6. **According to the passage, one reason that carbon dioxide increasingly builds up in the atmosphere is that:**

   F. the earth is heating up.

   G. there are not enough trees in our cities.

   H. the burning of fossil fuels releases $CO_2$.

   J. gases are trapped in the earth's atmosphere.

This question is about **cause-effect relationships**. To answer it correctly, you need to think about what causes the buildup of $CO_2$. It cannot be **F**, as the earth heating up is an effect of the buildup, not a cause. Both **G** and **J** may be true, but neither is a cause of increasing $CO_2$. **The best answer is H**; the second paragraph refers to "such human activity as burning of fossil fuels pumps [$CO_2$] into the atmosphere each year."

Copyright © American Book Company. DO NOT DUPLICATE. 1-888-264-5877.

7. **Considering the information provided in the passage, which of the following is the most accurate description of the $CO_2$ cycle?**

   A. The greenhouse effect produces carbon dioxide, $CO_2$ traps other gases, trees convert these gases to oxygen, and the burning of wood releases the oxygen into the atmosphere.

   B. Gases trap the earth's heat and produce the greenhouse effect, trees provide shade and $CO_2$ absorption, people release more $CO_2$, and more trees are needed to remove it from the atmosphere.

   C. Carbon dioxide traps the earth's heat, trees provide shade and remove $CO_2$, planting trees in urban areas removes great amounts of $CO_2$, and the earth's heat is decreased.

   D. Carbon dioxide is released into the atmosphere, trees absorb $CO_2$, they convert it into carbohydrates, and they release oxygen as a byproduct.

This **sequence of events** question asks about the order of the carbon dioxide cycle alluded to in the passage. None of the statements in Choice **A** is true. **B** describes a cycle of sorts, but it has none of the details necessary about what occurs in each step. **C** offers several facts which do no form a sequence. **The best answer is D.** Only Choice **D** provides an answer that is a logical sequence of events which is described as factual in the passage.

8. **According to the information in the passage, the greenhouse effect would decrease if:**

   I. more trees were planted.

   II. fewer fossil fuels were burned.

   III. more $CO_2$ remained in the atmosphere.

   F. I only

   G. II only

   H. I and II only

   J. I, II, and III

This is another question about **cause-effect relationships.** The information in Roman numeral I is correct because, according to the first paragraph, "Heat from the earth is held in our atmosphere by carbon dioxide" but "trees remove the $CO_2$ from the atmosphere." The information in Roman numeral II is also correct because, according to the second paragraph, "burning of fossil fuels pumps [$CO_2$] into the atmosphere." Roman numeral III, however, is incorrect because, again, according to the first paragraph, "Heat from the earth is held in our atmosphere by carbon dioxide," which means more $CO_2$ would produce more heat. Because Roman numeral III is incorrect, **J** cannot be the best answer. Because both Roman numerals I and II are correct, therefore, neither **F** nor **G** could be the best answer. **The best answer is H**.

Copyright © American Book Company. DO NOT DUPLICATE. 1-888-264-5877.

Read the chapters in this book for more tips about answering questions about various types of passages that you will see on the ACT Reading Test. Best of all, each chapter review will give you plenty of realistic ACT Reading Test questions to practice answering. Of course, don't forget about the diagnostic test at the beginning of the book and two practice tests at the end, each of which simulates a full ACT Reading Test.

---

## CHAPTER 1 SUMMARY

**Prose fiction** passages are short stories or excerpts from longer stories or novels.

There are two types of questions, **referring** (which are about facts clearly stated in the passage) and **reasoning** (which require deeper interpretation based on the passage). Each question also may address one or more of the following categories:

- **main ideas**
- **details**
- **sequence of events**
- **words and phrases in context**
- **comparisons and contrasts**
- **cause-effect relationships**
- **generalizations**
- **author's voice & method**

Within the **thirty-five minutes** allotted for the ACT Reading Test, you should give yourself an average of eight and a half minutes to read each passage and then answer the ten questions that follow it.

Copyright © American Book Company. DO NOT DUPLICATE. 1-888-264-5877.

Copyright © American Book Company. DO NOT DUPLICATE. 1-888-264-5877.

Copyright © American Book Company. DO NOT DUPLICATE. 1-888-264-5877.

# Chapter 2
# Reading for Understanding

Reading passages of different types—whether prose fiction, cultural essays, or scientific papers—provides a variety of experiences. The skills you develop by reading one kind of challenging text will translate into better and easier comprehension of other types.

For example, broadening your understanding of word meanings by reading biology and learning to process sequences of events by studying history will enhance your fiction reading ability. The kind of reader who excels on the ACT Reading Test can look through a passage in any genre and pinpoint main ideas, an event timeline, significant details, and working word definitions.

In this chapter, you'll review fundamentals to focus your comprehension skills and practice answering questions like those on the ACT Reading Test. The fundamentals of reading a passage for understanding include determining its **main idea**, finding and interpreting **significant details**, understanding the **sequence of events**, and finding **word meanings from context**.

## Main Idea

When reading a passage, you'll want to figure out its **main idea**—its essential or basic message. An author writes a passage in order to communicate an idea, and it is the reader's task to become aware of that idea. The passage's main idea may be directly stated by the author, or it may be implied.

In addition to finding the main idea of the passage, you will need to recognize the main idea of each supporting paragraph. This is an important part of comprehending any author's material. Main ideas in paragraphs will also be either directly stated or implied.

ACT Reading Test questions may use "main point" to refer to main idea. In prose fiction passages, "main conflict" or "main theme" may also be used. Whichever term you see, use the following strategies to answer main idea questions.

Copyright © American Book Company. DO NOT DUPLICATE. 1-888-264-5877.

# Directly Stated Main Idea

This kind of main idea is similar to the topic sentences you may have been instructed to include in your school writing; however, be aware that ACT Test passages rarely follow any kind of five paragraph format. If a passage has a directly stated main idea, you can best express the idea by quoting or rewording the most definitive portion of the passage.

Often, **directly stated main ideas** will be in the first or last paragraphs or at the beginning of significant body paragraphs. Also, remember to keep the title of the passage in mind, as it may help you determine whether the main idea is directly stated. A specific title may suggest a directly stated main idea, while a complicated or vague title can mean you'll need to do some detective work, which we'll discuss in the next section.

**To practice finding directly stated main ideas, read this passage, and answer the question.**

**SOCIAL SCIENCE:** This passage is adapted from "Equal Pay and Compensation Discrimination" by the Equal Employment Opportunity Commission.

1      The Equal Pay Act requires that men and women be given equal pay for equal work in the same establishment. The jobs need not be identical, but they must be substantially equal. It is job content, not job titles, that determines whether jobs are substantially equal. Specifically, the EPA states that employers may not pay unequal wages to men and
5      women who do equal work, or perform jobs that require substantially equal skill, effort, and responsibility, and that are performed under similar working conditions within the same establishment.

       Job skills are measured by factors like the experience, ability, education, and training required to perform the job. The key issue is what skills the job requires, not what skills
10     the individual employees may have. For example, two accounting jobs could be equal under the EPA even if one of the employees has a master's degree in physics, since that degree would not be required.

       The concept of responsibility is shown by the degree of accountability required in the job. For example, a salesperson who is delegated the duty of determining whether to
15     accept customers' personal checks has more responsibility than other salespeople. On the other hand, a minor step in responsibility, such as turning out the lights at 5:00, would not justify a pay differential.

### Which of the following best states the main idea of the passage?

**A.** The key issue is what skills the job requires, not what skills the individual employees may have.

**B.** The concept of responsibility is shown by the degree of accountability required in the job.

**C.** The Equal Pay Act requires that men and women be given equal pay for equal work in the same establishment.

**D.** It is job content, not job titles, that determines whether jobs are substantially equal.

Copyright © American Book Company. DO NOT DUPLICATE. 1-888-264-5877.

**The best answer is C.** This choice is directly stated in the first line of the passage. Don't be fooled by the phrase "the key issue" in Choice **A**, since the "key issue" it mentions is skill requirements for certain jobs, not employment equality. Choice **B** is a significant detail found in the third paragraph, but it only explains one aspect of the main idea. Choice **D** addresses a key element of the passage—job equality. But this sentence is not broad enough to represent the content of the whole passage; it doesn't even mention the Act itself.

| Tips for Finding a Directly Stated Main Idea |
|---|
| 1. **Read the title**. If a passage's main idea is directly stated, much of it may be included in the title. |
| 2. It may sound obvious, but it's essential to **read the entire passage**. You don't want to miss an important detail that might alter your choice. |
| 3. Before you look at the answer choices, **consider how you would state the main idea in your own words**. This will help you ignore any distracting information. |
| 4. **Re-read the most important details in each paragraph.** Many authors state their main ideas in introductions and conclusions. |
| 5. **Choose the best statement or restatement of the main idea.** If a choice contains key words from prominent sentences, part of the idea expressed in the title, and is supported by ideas from body paragraphs, the choice is likely the main idea. |

## IMPLIED MAIN IDEA

Other passages won't have clearly stated main ideas, but this doesn't mean they don't have them. Since the main idea in this kind of passage is implied, seek clues and hints by closely reading paragraphs. You will still want to use the techniques we just discussed, noting key words, titles, and phrases, but you'll need to summarize these things on your own. Read with focus, and identify the main idea before reading the choices.

Copyright © American Book Company. DO NOT DUPLICATE. 1-888-264-5877.

**To practice finding implied main ideas, read this passage, and answer the question.**

**SOCIAL SCIENCE:** This passage is adapted from *The Folklore of Plants* by T. F. Thiselton-Dyer.

1     Another anecdote current in Yorkshire is interesting, showing how fully superstitions of this kind are believed: A woman was lately in my shop, and in pulling out her purse brought out also a piece of stick a few inches long. I asked her why she carried that in her pocket.

5     "Oh," she replied, "I must not lose that, or I shall be done for."

    "Why so?" I inquired.

    "Well," she answered, "I carry that to keep off the witches; while I have that about me, they cannot hurt me."

    On my adding that there were no witches nowadays, she instantly replied, "Oh, yes!
10 There are thirteen at this very time in the town, but so long as I have my rowan-tree safe in my pocket they cannot hurt me."

**What main idea is the author trying to convey?**

**A.** The rowan-tree is renowned for its protection against witches.

**B.** All plants are believed to keep people safe from witchcraft.

**C.** Belief in the supernatural can lead people to develop protection against perceived evil.

**D.** Knowing the powers of each plant kept people safe from the malicious influences around them.

**The best answer is C.** Choice **C** is a good breakdown of the passage's main idea and is supported by each paragraph's details. Choice **A** supports the main idea, but it does not summarize the whole passage. There is no evidence in the passage to support the claim made in Choice **B**. Choice **D** is similar to Choice **B**; it uses convincing language, but its claim goes beyond what can be found in the passage.

| Tips for Determining an Implied Main Idea |
|---|
| 1.   **Read the title**. The title will help you identify the topic of the selection. |
| 2.   Again, **read the entire paragraph or passage**. In a good passage, every detail contributes to the development of the main idea. |
| 3.   Before you read the answer choices, **consider how you would state the main idea in your own words**. This will help you ignore any distracting information. |
| 4.   **Re-read the most important details in each paragraph.** Think of overall ideas they share in common. |
| 5.   To avoid choosing an answer that's almost correct, **rule out answers that only cover one part of the passage.** |

Copyright © American Book Company. DO NOT DUPLICATE. 1-888-264-5877.

## Practice 1: Main Ideas—Stated and Implied

Read the following passage, and answer the questions.

**NATURAL SCIENCE:** This passage is adapted from "Snakes on a Plane: The True Story" (©2008 American Book Company).

1   Guam's animal population was traditionally free of snakes, but air travel has changed that fact. The threat of imported snakes began shortly after World War II, when a few brown tree snakes got on board a United States military
5   transport plane from New Guinea. Soon, there was far more than a few snakes in Guam.

**Map of Guam**

This was a disaster for Guam. Though the brown tree snake population had been checked by wild boars in New Guinea, snakes entering Guam were uninhibited by natural
10   predators. This meant they were able to conquer and multiply as long as they stayed out of human sight, which was easy enough since these snakes are nocturnal. The brown tree snake is only slightly venomous and is mostly just an annoyance to humans. However, these snakes quickly eradicated Guam's natural bird species. In rare cases, they have
15   attempted to attack small children. While there have been no reports of death resulting from brown tree snake bites, the government posts warnings for citizens and tourists. These warnings caution parents to be aware of puncture wounds, lethargic behavior, and swelling in children's extremities.

Planes leaving Guam for the Hawaiian airport in Oahu must watch for slithering
20   stowaways that twine themselves around plane wheels for a free trip across the Pacific. Honolulu airport workers have learned to watch for these invasions, so they attempt to capture the nimble snakes before they can enter the island's dense vegetation. To the peril of Hawaii's beautiful bird populations, some snakes do escape. Hawaiian authorities have found far more dangerous snakes like boas and pythons, but these are very rare compared
25   to the threat of brown tree snakes. Airport security uses snake-sniffing dogs to check incoming planes for cold-blooded cargo. Even though some of these fugitives are just missing pets of reptile-loving islanders, Hawaii is at full alert for slithering Guamanian invaders.

**1. Which of the following best states the main idea of the passage?**

   **A.** Guam's animal population was traditionally free of snakes, but air travel has changed that fact.

   **B.** The threat of imported snakes began sometime after World War II, when a few brown tree snakes got on board a United States military transport plane from New Guinea.

   **C.** Carnivorous reptiles have traveled via airplane to islands throughout the Pacific.

   **D.** Imported species can be a real threat to island animal populations, especially where there are no natural predators.

Copyright © American Book Company. DO NOT DUPLICATE. 1-888-264-5877.

2. **The main point of the third paragraph is that:**

F. Hawaiian authorities have found far more dangerous snakes, but these are very rare compared to the threat of brown tree snakes.

G. Whether in Guam or Hawaii, the brown tree snake does irreparable damage to bird populations.

H. Hawaiian authorities are concerned about their islands becoming as overrun by brown tree snakes as Guam is.

J. Airports in Oahu have gotten very good at capturing brown tree snakes before the snakes can enter the island's vegetation.

# FINDING AND INTERPRETING SIGNIFICANT DETAILS

A common type of test question asks you to find a certain detail in a passage. Obviously, this can mean just about anything. Some detail questions are about plainly stated facts, but others involve your reasoning and an ability to connect the logic of multiple sentences. Reread a passage carefully if you are having trouble.

**To practice finding significant details, read this passage, and answer the question.**

**SOCIAL SCIENCE:** This passage is adapted from "Population and Food Supply" (©2008 American Book Company).

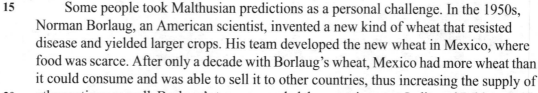

1    In 1798, British economist Thomas Malthus predicted that the disparity between the human species and the food supply would soon lead to massive starvation. Human populations were increasing rapidly,
5    while the food supply was increasing slowly. Malthus felt that populations would need to be prevented from growing somehow, or all would suffer. Malthus' ideas were popular and influenced thinkers from naturalist Charles Darwin to science fiction author Isaac Asimov.
10    Malthus also faced a variety of critics that ranged about as widely as possible. Both Karl Marx, who paved the way for socialism, and John Stuart Mill, who was a political economist in favor of free markets, attacked Malthus' assertions about the bad aspects of having more people around.

15    Some people took Malthusian predictions as a personal challenge. In the 1950s, Norman Borlaug, an American scientist, invented a new kind of wheat that resisted disease and yielded larger crops. His team developed the new wheat in Mexico, where food was scarce. After only a decade with Borlaug's wheat, Mexico had more wheat than it could consume and was able to sell it to other countries, thus increasing the supply of
20    other nations as well. Borlaug's team expanded the experiment to India and Pakistan with similar results. He has since won the Nobel Peace Prize and the United States' highest honors. According to multiple commentators, his innovation has saved almost a billion lives so far.

Copyright © American Book Company. DO NOT DUPLICATE. 1-888-264-5877.

**According to the passage, Thomas Malthus had an influence on all of the following fields EXCEPT:**

A. literature.

B. medicine.

C. economics.

D. natural science.

**The best answer is B.** Though Malthus' ideas likely influenced some doctors and medical scientists, this information is not mentioned in the passage. The key word in this question is "except." Don't forget to read every word in the question. In the passage it states that Malthus influenced Darwin (a natural scientist, which eliminates Choice **D**) and Asimov (an author, ruling out Choice **A**). Regarding Choice **C**, remember that influence can be positive or negative; this, Choice **C** doesn't work since Malthus inspired economists Mill and Marx to strongly disagree with him.

| **Tips for Finding and Determining Significant Details** |
|---|
| 1. Don't forget to **pay attention to everything.** |
| 2. **Note all proper nouns.** These tell who, which location, and what specific event may have been involved in an action. |
| 3. **Remember—sometimes you'll have to figure it out.** Some questions won't include choices that are lifted straight from the text. You'll have to think about how to work these questions out. |
| 4. **Use the tactics you learned for determining main ideas.** Since main ideas are supported by significant details, similar strategies can help you find them both. |

## Practice 2:   Significant Details

Answer the following questions based upon the last passage, "Population and Food Supply" on page 34.

1. **According to the passage, which of the following individuals provided the greatest refutation of Malthus' ideas about population and food supply?**

    A. Norman Borlaug

    B. Charles Darwin

    C. Karl Marx

    D. John Stuart Mill

Copyright © American Book Company. DO NOT DUPLICATE. 1-888-264-5877.

2. **According to the information in the passage, in order to prevent people from starving, Malthus most likely would have suggested:**

F. that people practice sexual abstinence.

G. that people emigrate to a more fertile region.

H. that methods to increase food production be practiced.

J. that people make a concerted effort to eat less.

# UNDERSTANDING SEQUENCE OF EVENTS

Questions dealing with **sequence of events** may appear simple, but you should be careful. Most passages follow a straightforward sequence; for example, most fiction passages present plot events in order from oldest to newest, and scientific journals order experiments from the first step to the last step.

However, some passages use sequences of events that are not so clear-cut. Think of a movie or TV show that moves back and forth in time. The important thing to keep in mind is that the sequence of events in a particular piece is not necessarily presented in order from earliest to latest or first to last. You must use evidence from the passage to choose the correct sequence of events.

**To practice understanding sequence of events, read this passage, and answer the question.**

**HUMANITIES:** This passage is adapted from "The Day the Music Died" (©2008 American Book Company).

1    On April 18, 1906, San Francisco was struck by an earthquake with the magnitude of 7.8 on the Richter scale. The quake only shook the city for about one minute, but it spawned fires that raged for the next four days and toppled many buildings. Among the buildings lost was the Palace Hotel. Constructed in 1875, the Palace became a treasured
5    local landmark, featuring tenor Enrico Caruso, the world's most popular singer at the time. After the 1906 quake, Caruso swore he would never return to San Francisco.

**According to the information in the passage, it can be inferred that Enrico Caruso's last concert at the Palace Hotel:**

A. took place before 1875.

B. took place after 1906.

C. took place between 1875 and 1906.

D. took place when the Palace Hotel was rebuilt.

Copyright © American Book Company. DO NOT DUPLICATE. 1-888-264-5877.

**The best answer is C.** Though it is a very wide range of dates, it is the only answer that the text proves. Since he performed at the hotel, which was built in 1875, **A** is not the answer. Choices **B** and **D** do not work since the passage does not suggest that he broke his vow to avoid San Francisco after the 1906 earthquake.

**Palace Hotel**

### Tips for Determining Sequence of Events

1. **Pay attention to transition words.** Sequences are clearer because of words like *first*, *next*, *therefore*, *then*, *after*, or *before*. There are many other transition words, so make sure you're familiar with them all.

2. **Note dates, times, seasons, and ages.** Anything that relates to measuring time is a clue you can use to establish sequence of events.

3. **Start from the main thread.** If a passage is confusingly jumping between present, future, and past, try to figure out which time period is the passage's main segment and which supplement it. For example, if a fiction passage about an adult includes a short flashback to the character's childhood, it may be helpful to read the flashback as if it's supportive of the basic story.

4. **Use common sense.** For example, when reading a passage about building a house, you already know that a foundation must be built well before the roof is added.

Copyright © American Book Company. DO NOT DUPLICATE. 1-888-264-5877.

## Practice 3:  Sequence of Events

**SOCIAL SCIENCE:** This passage is adapted from the National Archive's Eleanor Roosevelt Exhibit.

1    In a dramatic and celebrated act of conscience, Eleanor Roosevelt resigned from the Daughters of the American Revolution (DAR) when it barred the world-renowned singer Marian Anderson, an African
5    American, from performing at its Constitution Hall in Washington, D.C. Following this well-publicized controversy, the federal government invited Anderson to sing at a public recital on the steps of the Lincoln Memorial. On Easter Sunday, April 9, 1939, some
10    75,000 people came to hear the free recital. The incident put both the artist and the issue of racial discrimination in the national spotlight.

**Eleanor Roosevelt**

**Which of the following choices lists the events of the passage in the order in which they occurred?**

**A.** Eleanor Roosevelt resigns from the DAR, the federal government invites Marian Anderson to perform at Lincoln Memorial, Marian Anderson is barred from performing at Constitution Hall, the controversy is publicized.

**B.** Marian Anderson is barred from performing at Constitution Hall, the controversy is publicized, the federal government invites Marian Anderson to perform at Lincoln Memorial, Eleanor Roosevelt resigns from the DAR.

**C.** Marian Anderson is barred from performing at Constitution Hall, Eleanor Roosevelt resigns from the DAR, the controversy is publicized, the federal government invites Marian Anderson to perform at Lincoln Memorial.

**D.** The federal government invites Marian Anderson to perform at Lincoln Memorial, Marian Anderson is barred from performing at Constitution Hall, the controversy is publicized, Eleanor Roosevelt resigns from the DAR.

# FINDING WORD MEANING FROM CONTEXT

When a question asks about **word meaning**, you'll need to use the word's context to help you decide on the correct choice. Some questions will involve words with multiple common synonyms. To decide which is right for the sentence in question, rely on the clues you can find throughout the rest of the sentence, paragraph, and passage.

You can figure out words you're unfamiliar with in the same way. Try substituting each of the answer choices for the underlined word. This should rule out one or more incorrect answers and may even be all the help you need.

Copyright © American Book Company. DO NOT DUPLICATE. 1-888-264-5877.

**To practice finding word meaning, read the following paragraph, and answer the question.**

**HUMANITIES:** This passage is an excerpt from "On Interpretation" by Aristotle.

1       Spoken words are the symbols of mental experience, and written words are the symbols of spoken words. Just as all men have not the same writing, so all men have not the same speech sounds, but the mental experiences, which these directly symbolize, are the same for all, as also are those things of which our experiences are the images. This

5    matter has, however, been discussed in my treatise about the soul, for it belongs to an investigation distinct from that which lies before us.

**What does the author mean by his use of the word *treatise*?**

**A.** peace agreement

**B.** comedy

**C.** discussion

**D.** dreams

**The best answer is C.** To write "discussed in my discussion" would be repetitive and boring, but it would make sense. The word *treatise* sounds a lot like *treaty*, which is a peace agreement, but the two words mean different things, so Choice **A** is incorrect. Read the sentence in question again; do you see how inserting "peace agreement" doesn't work? Choice **B** is also incorrect since the author describes the matter as "an investigation," and comic theater is not the most frequent method of investigating philosophical things. Choice **D** is incorrect; though the author may or may not dream "about the soul," the author's readers have no way of viewing his dreams.

| Tips for Determining Word Meaning from Context |
| --- |
| 1.  **Substitute answer choices for the word in question,** and see which one best fits into the sentence. |
| 2.  **Rule out choices that are definitely incorrect.** In most questions, there will only be two or three choices that seem like possible correct answers. |
| 3.  **Re-read the word's surrounding sentence, paragraph, or passage.** |
| 4.  **Keep the author's dialect in mind.** An author from eighteenth century London and an author from modern New Orleans may use varying definitions of the same words. |

Copyright © American Book Company. DO NOT DUPLICATE. 1-888-264-5877.

## Practice 4:  Word Meaning from Context

**HUMANITIES:** This passage is adapted from "How to Tell a Story" by Mark Twain.

1       The humorous story is told gravely; the teller does his best to conceal the fact that he even dimly suspects that there is anything funny about it; but the teller of the comic story tells you beforehand that it is one of the funniest things he has ever heard, then tells it with eager delight, and is the first person to laugh when he gets through. And

5    sometimes, if he has had good success, he is so glad and happy that he will repeat the nub of it and glance around from face to face, collecting applause, and then repeat it again. It is a pathetic thing to see.

1. **What is the best synonym for the word *dimly*, as used in line 2?**

    **A.** darkly

    **B.** insightfully

    **C.** slightly

    **D.** wittily

2. **Which of these best expresses the meaning of the word *nub*, as used in line 5?**

    **F.** title and main idea

    **G.** least offensive part

    **H.** round lump on a tree

    **J.** most popular part

---

### CHAPTER 2 SUMMARY

The fundamentals of reading a passage for understanding include determining its **main idea**, finding and interpreting **significant details**, understanding the **sequence of events**, and finding **word meanings from context**.

- The **main idea** is the central point of the passage and can be directly stated or implied.

- **Supporting details** are the key elements used in the passage to support the point.

- **Sequence of events** is the order in which things happen in the passage.

- Finding **word meaning from context** is using the evidence around an unfamiliar word to determine its meaning.

Copyright © American Book Company. DO NOT DUPLICATE. 1-888-264-5877.

# CHAPTER 2 REVIEW

**PROSE FICTION:** This passage is adapted from *A House of Gentlefolk* by Ivan Turgenev. In this novel, the town's name has been intentionally rewritten as "O——."

1    The name of the young man whom we have just introduced to the reader was Vladimir Nikolaitch Panshin. He served in Petersburg on special
5    commissions in the department of internal affairs. He had come to the town of O—— to carry out some temporary government commissions, and was in attendance on the Governor-
10   General Zonnenberg, to whom he happened to be distantly related.

     Panshin's father, a retired cavalry officer and a notorious gambler, was a man with insinuating eyes, a battered
15   countenance, and a nervous twitch about the mouth. He spent his whole life hanging about the aristocratic world; frequented the English clubs of both capitals, and had the reputation of
20   a smart, not very trustworthy, but jolly good-natured fellow. In spite of his smartness, he was almost always on the brink of ruin, and the property he left his son was small and heavily
25   encumbered. To make up for that, however, he did exert himself, after his own fashion, over his son's education.

     Vladimir Nikolaitch spoke French very well, English well, and German
30   badly; that is the proper thing; fashionable people would be ashamed to speak German well; but to utter an occasional—generally a humorous— phrase in German is quite correct, *c'est*
35   *mâme très chic,* as the Parisians of Petersburg express themselves. By the time he was fifteen, Vladimir knew how to enter any drawing-room

40   without embarrassment, how to move about in it gracefully and to leave it at the appropriate moment.

     Panshin's father gained many connections for his son. He never lost an opportunity, while shuffling the
45   cards between two rubbers, or playing a successful trump, of dropping a hint about his Volodka to any personage of importance who was a devotee of cards. And Vladimir, too, during his
50   residence at the university, which he left without a very brilliant degree, formed an acquaintance with several young men of quality, and gained an entry into the best houses.

55   He was received cordially everywhere: he was very good-looking, easy in his manners, amusing, always in good health, and ready for everything; respectful, when he ought
60   to be; insolent, when he dared to be; excellent company, *un charmant garçon.* The promised land lay before him. Panshin quickly learnt the secret of getting on in the world; he knew how
65   to yield with genuine respect to its decrees; he knew how to take up trifles with half ironical seriousness, and to appear to regard everything serious as trifling; he was a capital dancer; and
70   dressed in the English style. In a short time he gained the reputation of being one of the smartest and most attractive young men in Petersburg.

     Panshin was indeed very smart, not
75   less so than his father; but he was also very talented. He did everything well; he sang charmingly, sketched with spirit, wrote verses, and was a very fair actor. He was only twenty-eight, and he
80   was already a *kammer-yunker,* and had a very good position. Panshin had

Copyright © American Book Company. DO NOT DUPLICATE. 1-888-264-5877.

complete confidence in himself, in his own intelligence, and his own penetration; he made his way with
85 light-hearted assurance, everything went smoothly with him. He was used to being liked by everyone, old and young, and imagined that he understood people, especially women:
90 he certainly understood their ordinary weaknesses.

As a man of artistic leanings, he was conscious of a capacity for passion, for being carried away, even
95 for enthusiasm, and, consequently, he permitted himself various irregularities; he was dissipated, associated with persons not belonging to good society, and, in general,
100 conducted himself in a free and easy manner; but at heart he was cold and false, and at the moment of the most boisterous revelry his sharp brown eye was always alert, taking everything in.
105 This bold, independent young man could never forget himself and be completely carried away. To his credit it must be said, that he never boasted of his conquests.

110 He had found his way into Marya Dmitrievna's house immediately he arrived in O——, and was soon perfectly at home there. Marya Dmitrievna absolutely adored him.
115 Panshin exchanged cordial greetings with everyone in the room; he shook hands with Marya Dmitrievna and Lisaveta Mihalovna, clapped Gedeonovsky lightly on the shoulder,
120 and turning round on his heels, put his hand on Lenotchka's head and kissed her on the forehead.

1. **When the author states the property that Panshin's father left to Panshin was "heavily encumbered" (lines 24 and 25), he most likely means:**

   A. the property was burdened by financial obligations.

   B. the property was overgrown with weeds.

   C. it was a very long ordeal to locate the property on a map.

   D. the property was not well maintained or protected.

2. **What statement most closely describes the main insight of the second paragraph (lines 12–27)?**

   F. Panshin's father was known to be an alcoholic.

   G. Though Panshin's father had shortcomings, he made sure Panshin had an education.

   H. Panshin's father kept the wrong company and, therefore, eventually lost all of his money.

   J. Though Panshin's father was a jolly, good-natured fellow, he was an alcoholic.

3. **As it is used in its context, the term *insolent* (line 60), most nearly means:**

   A. sarcastic.

   B. arrogant.

   C. without compassion.

   D. loud.

Copyright © American Book Company. DO NOT DUPLICATE. 1-888-264-5877.

4. **It is reasonable to infer from the passage that the reason Panshin "speaks German badly" is that:**

   F. learning German is time-consuming.

   G. he has not been taught German.

   H. he hates Germany.

   J. it helps him to fit in.

5. **According to the description of his character in the passage, if Panshin were to win a contest (of any sort), what would his LEAST likely reaction be?**

   A. to brag about it to his friends

   B. to jump up and down in celebration

   C. to share the news with his father

   D. to feel a sense of accomplishment

6. **Based on the characteristics presented in the passage, which of the following scenarios would fit the personality of Panshin's father?**

  I. Panshin's father would gamble away a large sum of money.

  II. Panshin's father would be found mingling only with people from high society.

  III. Panshin's father would refrain from boasting about receiving a promotion.

   F. I only

   G. III only

   H. I and II only

   J. I, II, and III

7. **In the first two sentences of the fourth paragraph (lines 42–49), what might the author be implying about the priorities of Panshin's father?**

   A. Gambling and finding connections for his son seem equally important to Panshin's father.

   B. Getting contacts for Panshin is his father's favorite excuse for gambling.

   C. Panshin's father uses gambling as an excuse for helping Panshin gain new connections.

   D. Panshin's father does not really seem to care about gambling or helping his son.

8. **According to the fifth paragraph, which of the following is NOT a secret of "getting on in the world" used by Panshin?**

   F. Pretend that unimportant things are important.

   G. Pretend that important things are not important.

   H. Become a great dancer.

   J. Dress like a high-class Russian.

9. **Concerning Panshin, what might one infer to be the reason that "at heart he was cold and false" (lines 101–102)?**

   A. He wishes to maintain self-control.

   B. He is not a creative or passionate person.

   C. He lacks self-confidence.

   D. He is bitter about this father's influence on his life.

Copyright © American Book Company. DO NOT DUPLICATE. 1-888-264-5877.

10. **According to the passage, what was one of the direct results of Panshin's formal education?**

    F.  He left without a very brilliant degree.

    G.  He was received cordially everywhere.

    H.  The promised land lay before him.

    J.  He was considered one of the most attractive young men in Petersburg.

Copyright © American Book Company. DO NOT DUPLICATE. 1-888-264-5877.

# Chapter 3
# Critical Reading

After developing an understanding of a written passage, the next step is to apply **critical reading**. This means reading a passage actively and thoughtfully, looking for ways to analyze complex relationships between characters and events, the author's writing style, methods the author uses to communicate arguments, and so on. Also, you'll need to be able to summarize each part of a passage.

In this chapter, you can practice your critical reading skills by working with the same kinds of passages that the ACT Reading Test features. Critical reading includes examining **comparative relationships** and **cause-effect relationships**, making **generalizations** based on a passage, and analyzing the **author's voice and method**.

## COMPARATIVE RELATIONSHIPS

These questions are about **comparing and contrasting** passage elements, including opinions, characters, and terms. You'll need to be able to pick out key differences between two otherwise similar excerpts from a passage; this is called contrasting.

You should also practice comparing, or finding common qualities between different parts of a passage. These kinds of questions will test your logic and ability to construct a short analysis of passage components.

Copyright © American Book Company. DO NOT DUPLICATE. 1-888-264-5877.

**To practice comparative relationships, read this passage, and answer the questions**.

**PROSE FICTION:** The passage is adapted from "After the Theatre," a short story by Anton Chekhov (1860–1904).

1    Nadya Zelenin had just come back with her mamma from the theatre where she had seen a performance of *Yevgeny Onyegin*. As soon as she reached her own room she threw off her dress, let down her hair, and in her petticoat and white dressing-jacket hastily sat down to the table to write a letter like Tatyana's.

5    "I love you," she wrote, "but you do not love me, do not love me!"

She wrote it and laughed.

She was only sixteen and did not yet love anyone. She knew that an officer called Gorny and a student called Gruzdev loved her, but now after the opera she wanted to be doubtful of their love. To be unloved and unhappy—how interesting that was. There is
10    something beautiful, touching, and poetical about it when one loves and the other is indifferent. Onyegin was interesting because he was not in love at all, and Tatyana was fascinating because she was so much in love; but if they had been equally in love with each other and had been happy, they would perhaps have seemed dull.

"Leave off declaring that you love me," Nadya went on writing, thinking of Gorny.
15    "I cannot believe it. You are very clever, cultivated, serious, you have immense talent, and perhaps a brilliant future awaits you, while I am an uninteresting girl of no importance, and you know very well that I should be only a hindrance in your life. It is true that you were attracted by me and thought you had found your ideal in me, but that was a mistake, and now you are asking yourself in despair: 'Why did I meet that girl?' And only your
20    goodness of heart prevents you from owning it to yourself…"

1.   **Based on her letter to Gorny, Nadya wants Gorny to feel the same way toward her that:**

   **A.** she feels toward him.

   **B.** Gruzdev feels toward her.

   **C.** Onyegin feels toward Tatyana.

   **D.** Tatyana feels toward Onyegin.

**The best answer is C**. Nadya wants to have a relationship with someone that imitates the one she's just witnessed at the theatre. In her letter, she is pretending to love Gorny. If the relationship she desires is to be complete, then he must express indifference toward her love. In her letter, she is encouraging his indifference. She wants Gorny to feel toward her like Onyegin feels toward Tatyana in the play (**C**). She does not want her significant other to return her love. Choice **A** is wrong because, in her letter, she declares to Gorny, "I love you," but then she discourages his love for her. Choice **B** is incorrect because lines 7 and 8 state that she knew "a student called Gruzdev loved her"; that's not what she wants either. And similarly, Choice **D** is incorrect because line 12 tells us that Tatyana was in love.

Copyright © American Book Company. DO NOT DUPLICATE. 1-888-264-5877.

This kind of question tests your ability to compare. Now, let's take a look at an example of a contrast question using the same passage.

2. **After seeing a performance of *Yevgeny Onyegin*, Nadya thinks, "to be unloved and unhappy—how interesting that was." If this were true, which of the characters mentioned would be leading an "interesting" life?**

    I. Nadya

    II. Gorney

    III. Gruzdev

    **A.** I only

    **B.** II only

    **C.** I and II

    **D.** II and III

**The best answer is D**. The key to the answer lies in the contrast between the way things really are and the way Nadya wishes they would be. Line 7 states that Nadya "did not yet love anyone." The next sentence states that "an officer called Gorny and a student called Gruzdev loved her." Nadya may not realize that she is experiencing what she describes in lines 9 and 10 "There is something beautiful, touching, and poetical about it when one loves and the other is indifferent." The only problem is that she is the one who is indifferent; she'd prefer to be the one in love. Roman numeral I is eliminated; Roman numeral II and III remain.

---

| **Tips for Evaluating Comparative Relationships** |
| --- |
| 1. **Look for common ground**, especially between two things that seem to be different. |
| 2. **Alternately, look for distinguishing traits**, especially between two things that seem to be very similar. |
| 3. **Pay attention as you read.** Look for the individual elements of each piece of the passage. |
| 4. **Look for the hidden comparisons**, not just the obvious ones. |
| 5. **Consider the author's point of view.** By using a different perspective, you may be able to see relationships you hadn't thought about. |

Copyright © American Book Company. DO NOT DUPLICATE. 1-888-264-5877.

## Practice 1: Comparative Relationships

**NATURAL SCIENCE:** This passage is adapted from "Stimulating Nerve Cells to Treat Injuries" (American Book Company © 2008).

1      Spinal cord injury can have tragic and often permanent results. It often leads to partial or full paralysis, with victims losing sensation and/or movement in part or all of the body. Scientists and doctors once believed that the vast majority of these injuries could not be overcome. New research, however, provides hope for the future.

5      The spinal cord, which runs the length of the back and has the consistency of toothpaste, cannot simply be repaired by surgery when damaged or cut. Unlike other body cells, the cells of the brain and spinal cord do not heal by replacing themselves when injured. When a person cuts his finger, for example, his or her skin eventually heals. The nerves in the finger can heal themselves as well, though the healing process is different.

10      Doctors and researchers once believed that, when the nerves of the brain and spinal cord gained maturity, they could never divide again. Recently, however, scientists have discovered that some cells in the central nervous system can be stimulated to divide to form new nerve cells. This exciting discovery has given many people hope that one day the spinal cord can be stimulated to heal itself after injury. Researchers are now exploring
15  drugs which may promote nerve growth and healing. They are also exploring the possibility of treating the injuries with nervous tissue transplants. In the meantime, physical therapy has been partially effective in restoring some sensation and movement in injury victims, and drugs are administered soon after an injury to help limit the damage.

1. **According to the passage, how are skin cells different than spinal cord cells?**

   **A.** Skin cells naturally heal themselves, but spinal cord cells do not.

   **B.** Skin cells contain nerves, but spinal cord cells do not.

   **C.** Skin cells can divide to form new cells, but spinal cord cells cannot.

   **D.** Actually, skin cells are NOT different than spinal cord cells.

2. **According to the passage, future treatments of spinal cord injuries could include all of the following EXCEPT:**

   **F.** the use of drugs.

   **G.** the transplant of nervous tissue.

   **H.** the discontinuance of physical therapy.

   **J.** the stimulation of new nerve cell growth.

Copyright © American Book Company. DO NOT DUPLICATE. 1-888-264-5877.

# CAUSE-EFFECT RELATIONSHIPS

The meaning of the term cause-effect is pretty simple; it's the pairing of a cause with the effect it has. On the ACT Reading Test, these questions will present you with either a cause or an effect and ask you to determine the other. You'll be asked to locate examples of this relationship in both fiction and nonfiction passages. For example, events in a short story can set up unexpected later results. Much like comparison relationships, you'll often have to connect pieces on your own, as **cause-effect relationships** are sometimes not directly stated.

**To practice cause-effect, read the following passage, and answer the question.**

**PROSE FICTION:** This passage is adapted from *The Insurgent* by Ludovic Halévy, published in 1907.

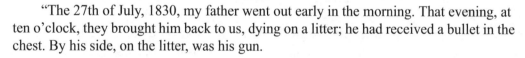

1    "Prisoner," said the president of the military tribunal, "have you anything to add in  your own defense?"

    "Yes, Colonel," answered the prisoner.
5    "You assigned me a little lawyer who has defended me in his fashion. I want to defend myself in my own. My name is Martin,— Louis Joseph. I'm fifty-five. My father was a locksmith. He had a little shop up in the St.
10    Martin quarter, and he had only a little business. We were able to live. I learned to read in the *National,* which was, I believe, Monsieur Thiers's newspaper.

    "The 27th of July, 1830, my father went out early in the morning. That evening, at ten o'clock, they brought him back to us, dying on a litter; he had received a bullet in the
15    chest. By his side, on the litter, was his gun.

    "'Take it,' he said to me; 'I give it to you,—and whenever there shall be an insurrection against the government,—always, always, always!'

    "An hour after he was dead. I went out into the night. At the first barricade, I stopped and offered myself. A man examined me by the light of a lantern. 'A child,' he cried. I
20    was not yet fifteen. I was very small, very undersized. I answered, 'A child, that's possible; but my father was killed two hours ago. He gave me his gun. Teach me how to use it.'

    "From that moment I became what I have always been for forty years—an insurgent! If I fought under the Commune, it was not because I was forced for the thirty cents. It was
25    from liking, for pleasure, by habit, by routine."

Copyright © American Book Company. DO NOT DUPLICATE. 1-888-264-5877.

**Why is the prisoner on trial?**

**A.** for revolting against the established political authority

**B.** for running his father's illegal business

**C.** for taking revenge for his father's death

**D.** for abandonment of his military duties

**The best answer is A.** The prisoner is on trial before a military tribunal, which is a military court created to try individuals who are enemy forces during wartime or have acted in an illegal manner. The title of the short story is also a major clue. There is no evidence in the passage to support Choices **B** or **D**. Choice **C** may be a true statement, but revenge is not a crime that can be tried or a reason for arrest. It is not the direct cause of his arrest. Direct causes are supported by concrete information in the passage.

| Tips for Evaluating Cause-Effect Relationships |
| --- |
| 1. **A cause must come before an effect**, so use your knowledge of sequence of events. |
| 2. **Find evidence in the passage** that proves the pair of events is related. |
| 3. **Look for hidden comparisons**, not just the obvious ones. |
| 4. **Consider the author's point of view.** By using a different perspective, you may be able to see relationships you hadn't thought about. |

## Practice 2:   Cause-Effect Relationships

Refer to the passage adapted from *The Insurgent* by Ludovic Halévy on the previous page.

1. **Other than "from liking, for pleasure, by habit, by routine," why did the prisoner most likely fight as an insurgent?**

   **A.** because of his father's wishes

   **B.** because he was getting old

   **C.** because he was trained by other insurgents

   **D.** because the government was oppressive

Copyright © American Book Company. DO NOT DUPLICATE. 1-888-264-5877.

**2. Why was the prisoner's father killed?**

   **F.** for being out past curfew

   **G.** for carrying a firearm

   **H.** for fighting as an insurgent

   **J.** for no apparent reason

# GENERALIZATIONS

To generalize means to draw a conclusion from detailed information. The key to excelling at **generalization** questions is using a skill you probably use every day—the ability to accurately and thoroughly make inferences. If you go out to a restaurant and your date is yawning, checking her watch, and sending text messages during your meal, you can infer that she is bored. The generalization that someone acting in this way is not enjoying herself and would rather go home is based on the detailed information presented to you, which adheres to general behavior that you may have observed in the past.

The ACT Reading Test will measure your abilities to draw conclusions on a variety of subjects from the traits of fiction characters to architecture criticism.

**To practice making generalizations, read the following passage, and answer the question.**

**HUMANITIES:** This passage is adapted from "How Riley Became King" (©2008 American Book Company).

1      Riley B. King and his guitar turned up in Memphis in 1948. Upon landing a job as a singer at Memphis' R&B radio station, he started cutting records for a small label. Legendary
5      producer Sam Phillips, who later launched the careers of music greats Elvis Presley and Johnny Cash, worked on King's songs. King became a local DJ with the nickname "Beale Street Blues Boy," eventually trimmed to just "B. B."

10     During the '50s, B. B. King was among the biggest names in blues, racking up an impressive array of R&B hits. By 1962, Frank Sinatra, still one of the most popular artists in the world, had taken an interest in King's career, helping the bluesman book high-profile concerts in Las Vegas.

15     King made his name outside the blues world with his Grammy winning 1969 remake of "The Thrill is Gone," originally by singer Roy Hawkins. King's highly polished update was a surprising pop hit and placed #183 in *Rolling Stone* magazine's *Top 500 Songs of All Time*. He parlayed his new popularity with rock fans into a spot on The Rolling Stones' colossal 1969 tour. King's mainstream success continued, though he remained
20     more popular in his original market, placing songs on the R&B charts seventy-four times by the end of the '70s.

Copyright © American Book Company. DO NOT DUPLICATE. 1-888-264-5877.

**King's legendary musical status came from his ability to:**

I. remain relevant in the industry for over three decades.

II. team up with highly influential people in the music world.

III. remix songs and produce hits.

A. I only

B. II only

C. I and II only

D. I, II, and III

**The best answer is C**. The details of the passage support both Roman numerals I and II. The passage states that he did remix "The Thrill is Gone," but this fact is not enough to infer that this was an ongoing activity; this eliminates Roman numeral III.

| Tips for Evaluating Generalizations |
|---|
| 1. **Use the skills you practiced while working on main ideas.** The main difference will be that generalization questions involve parts of passages, not whole passages. |
| 2. **Your goal is to briefly and effectively summarize a passage** element, so don't get distracted; pay the most attention to the most important aspects. |
| 3. **Develop your answer** before reading the answer choices. This will keep you from settling on a wrong answer that sounds pretty close. |
| 4. **Eliminate choices that contain obviously wrong information.** Usually, one or more answer choices will stand out immediately as false thanks to your critical reading of the passage. |
| 5. **Consider how you'd summarize the passage** if it were a popular movie or book. This may help you put your summary into words. |

Copyright © American Book Company. DO NOT DUPLICATE. 1-888-264-5877.

## Practice 3: Generalizations

Refer to the passage adapted from "How Riley Became King" on page 51.

1. **Which of these was the most popular form of music in America during the 1960s?**

   A. blues

   B. R&B

   C. rock

   D. Johnny Cash's

2. **What was the city of Memphis most likely known for in the 1940s and '50s?**

   F. talented young musicians

   G. Frank Sinatra

   H. the R&B charts

   J. *Rolling Stone* magazine

# AUTHOR'S VOICE AND METHOD

**Voice** refers to an author's writing style. This involves things like use of figurative and descriptive language, tone, and mood. **Method** includes how the passage works and how the author accomplishes a purpose. Organization and construction of arguments are included in method.

**To practice interpreting author's voice and method, read this passage, and answer the questions.**

**SOCIAL SCIENCE:** This passage is adapted from John F. Kennedy's Inaugural Address.

1      In the long history of the world, only a few generations have been granted the role of defending freedom in its hour of maximum danger. I do not shrink from this responsibility—I welcome it. I do not believe that any of us would exchange places with any other people or any other generation. The energy, the faith, the devotion which we
5      bring to this endeavor will light our country and all who serve it. And the glow from that fire can truly light the world. And so, my fellow Americans, ask not what your country can do for you; ask what you can do for your country. My fellow citizens of the world, ask not what America will do for you, but what together we can do for the freedom of man.

Copyright © American Book Company. DO NOT DUPLICATE. 1-888-264-5877.

1. **What is the primary purpose for Kennedy's repeating the words "my fellow," "ask not what," "can do for," and "ask what," in the last two sentences of the passage?**

   A. to make sure his audience hears him

   B. to emphasize his call to action

   C. to redirect the thinking of his audience

   D. to make his speech memorable

**The best answer is B.** Though Kennedy most likely intended to achieve all of these options, his primary goal was to call for citizens to act. Choice **A** is not likely because the repeated words contain two distinct messages, not the same message twice. Choices **C** and **D** are desirable outcomes of the speech, but for these to happen the call to action must first be heard and understood.

This question referred to the author's use of voice; the next question will concern the passage's method.

2. **What is most likely the author's intended meaning of "ask not what your country can do for you; ask what you can do for your country"?**

   F. Don't expect freedom to be an easy thing to keep.

   G. We can cut taxes and fight wars at the same time.

   H. Citizens should be servants of their countries, not the other way around.

   J. Never ask questions about doing things for other people.

**The best answer is F.** From the beginning of the passage, the author discusses his belief in the virtues and challenges of defending freedom, indicating that he feels it is a personal responsibility of all citizens. **G** is incorrect; taxes aren't mentioned in the passage, but, perhaps more importantly, the passage makes clear that individual sacrifice is supposed to be critical. **H** and **J** may sound like straight interpretations of the line, but these choices do not take into account the rest of the passage, which shows that the author is advocating his view of freedom, not mandatory service.

| Tips for Analyzing Author's Voice and Method |
| --- |
| 1. **Think about how the author is different** from other authors. Does the author use more or less formal language (or quotations, statistics, dialogue, etc.) than other authors? |
| 2. **Think** about how the argument is constructed. |
| 3. **Consider the author's intent.** This can help you determine why the author used certain language. |

Copyright © American Book Company. DO NOT DUPLICATE. 1-888-264-5877.

## Practice 4: Author's Voice and Method

Refer to the passage adapted from John F. Kennedy's Inaugural Address on page 53.

1. **Which words does the author use metaphorically in lines 4–6? ("The energy, the faith, the devotion which we bring to this endeavor will light our country and all who serve it. And the glow from that fire can truly light the world.")**

   A. our country and all who serve it

   B. faith

   C. energy and devotion

   D. light and fire

2. **What does the author most likely mean by "light the world"?**

   F. provide electricity

   G. work effectively

   H. spread freedom

   J. spread Christianity

3. **Judging by the tone of this excerpt of the speech, President Kennedy felt:**

   A. saddened that Americans did not want to fight for freedom.

   B. inspired about the opportunity to uphold freedom.

   C. anxious about the coming conflicts.

   D. excited about going to war.

Copyright © American Book Company. DO NOT DUPLICATE. 1-888-264-5877.

# CHAPTER 3 SUMMARY

Critical reading includes examining **comparative relationships** and **cause-effect relationships**, making **generalizations** based on a passage, and analyzing the **author's voice and method**.

- **Comparative relationships** are points of similarity or distinction between two related elements of a passage.

- In a **cause-effect relationship**, one part of a passage "causes" another.

- **Generalizations** are used to summarize the key points of something in a passage.

- **Author's voice** refers to writing style, while **author's method** means the ways the author chooses to construct arguments or stories.

Copyright © American Book Company. DO NOT DUPLICATE. 1-888-264-5877.

# CHAPTER 3 REVIEW

**SOCIAL SCIENCE:** This passage is adapted from "Political Campaigning, as Described by a Disgruntled Voter" (©2008 American Book Company).

1    Political campaigning can be messy because candidates usually have conflicting stances on issues. To set themselves apart, candidates use a
5    variety of strategies in their hunt for votes. Some are meant to highlight a candidate's more popular aspects, but campaigns can become rough when candidates resort to tactics designed
10    instead to undermine each other.

When the gloves come off and candidates begin accusing and lying about each other, this is called negative campaigning; name calling and
15    mudslinging are two of its more common types. Name calling is considered harmful and immature when conducted on the playground but witty and courageous in a presidential
20    campaign. Candidates use it because it is direct and can be tricky to disprove, saddling an opponent with a stigma that may not be based on fact. Mudslinging is more advanced than name calling,
25    involving broad accusations that quickly become exaggerated and mean-spirited. A mudslinging candidate may claim that his or her opponent breaks promises, has helped
30    shady special interest groups, has an untrustworthy voting record, or kicks local puppies.

Perhaps the most crucial element of negative campaigning is the fear factor.
35    A political candidate using this method seeks to stir a general panic and dread in voters by claiming that a vote for his or her opponent would guarantee

40    immediately startling results, like higher taxes, a terrorist invasion, or a new military draft. According to many candidates, the only thing we have to fear is everything the opposing candidate has ever stood for.

45    The bandwagon approach is similar, referring to a candidate's attempts to persuade voters by implying, "The majority is voting for me; therefore, it stands to reason that you should too." A
50    comment like this may be supported by some sort of favorable opinion poll. This method of persuasion can work well, as some people fear being seen as out of step with their peers, anti-
55    progress, or left out of the crowd. Spin, a similar campaign tactic, involves citing a set of apparent facts that has been meticulously groomed to present only certain information about a
60    situation. Using the spin tactic, the candidate either ignores or discredits critics as unpatriotic, racist, short-sighted, or any available inflammatory charge within some semblance of logic.

65    Unfortunately, negative campaigning seems to benefit politicians, even though voters claim frustration with and fatigue from the barrage of bickering, fairytales, and
70    insults. The evidence that rudeness and bold deceit can sometimes help a campaign is what encourages so many candidates to assault both the truth and each other.

75    Politicians may use some relatively positive ploys to sway pliable voters, such as endorsements from famous or influential people. Endorsements are apparently more effective when given
80    by well-liked politions, CEOs, or

Copyright © American Book Company. DO NOT DUPLICATE. 1-888-264-5877.

"public figures." Movie stars and musicians sometimes give endorsements, but this only annoys
85 most people. The endorser likely believes that if the candidate is elected, both of them will look good. Another non-negative and widely used tactic is the "plain ol' folks" approach.
90 Candidates try to act like normal people by wearing jeans, offensively copying regional dialect, and voicing concerns about ordinary, day-to-day, working person's struggles.

95 Since the majority rules in a democracy, most candidates go out of their way to emphasize the issues on which they agree with the biggest crowd of voters. Some examples are
100 immigration laws and environmental issues. Immigration laws could mean leniency toward immigration or tougher restrictions on how many people are allowed to enter the country.
105 This is an especially polarizing issue, so politicians have to choose carefully. Environmental issues might become a concern for a property owner wanting to sell land to developers; if
110 construction would impact nearby wetlands, affecting the ecosystem, a conflict could occur. Voters in this community would want to know how a candidate, if elected, would deal with
115 the situation; therefore, to maximize appeal to voters, the candidate may just reword and repeat whatever the most people seem to be saying.

Some campaigns that use these
120 techniques can be run so successfully that they develop significant leads over their opponents. Voters may transfer their association with one candidate or party to the other because of
125 campaigns. Opinions and feelings

toward candidates can change during the process, amid all the clever deception and brutal smears on reputations, which is why having a
130 good campaign strategy is so crucial to winning an election.

1. **In terms of developing the passage, the fifth paragraph (lines 66–75) primarily serves to:**
   A. transition between negative and positive campaigning.
   B. transition between politicians and political endorsers.
   C. contradict the argument presented in the first half of the passage.
   D. introduce the portion of the passage dedicated to positive campaigning.

2. **If saying that a political opponent is a *flip-flopper* is an example of name calling, then an example of mudslinging would be to say that the same opponent:**
   F. is a warmonger.
   G. cannot be trusted to fulfill any promises he has made.
   H. has taken one side of an issue then changed his mind.
   J. does not clearly state where he stand on issues.

3. **What word would best describe the tone of the author in this passage?**
   A. absurd
   B. hopeless
   C. sarcastic
   D. austere

Copyright © American Book Company. DO NOT DUPLICATE. 1-888-264-5877.

4. **According to the seventh paragraph (lines 95–118), in order for candidates to win voter support on an issue that concerns the majority, they must:**

   I. support environmentalism.

   II. oppose immigration.

   III. support the popular side of an issue.

   F. I only

   G. II only

   H. III only

   J. I and II only

5. **An example of an endorsement would be:**

   A. a celebrity appearing at a campaign fundraiser.

   B. a private citizen saying the candidate was helpful in the past.

   C. a fellow politician offering thoughts on an issue.

   D. television ads attacking an opponent.

6. **The "rudeness and bold deceit" in lines 71 and 72 refer in this instance to:**

   F. voter behavior at the polls.

   G. how political candidates behave with their families.

   H. tactics of negative campaigning.

   J. poor standards of political endorsements.

7. **According to the passage, which of the following are reasons candidates use negative campaigning?**

   I. It seems to benefit their campaign.

   II. It guarantees the most endorsements.

   III. It is better to do unto others before they do unto you.

   A. I only

   B. III only

   C. I and II only

   D. I, II, and III

8. **According to the last paragraph, why do candidates lose elections?**

   I. because their opponents run better campaigns than they do

   II. because their opponents are more qualified

   III. because their opponents change their political affiliations

   F. I only

   G. III only

   H. I and II only

   J. I, II, and III

9. **According to the passage, which of the following is true about political endorsements?**

   A. Everyone will believe an endorsement.

   B. Some endorsements annoy the voters.

   C. They most often backfire.

   D. Most candidates agree not to use them.

Copyright © American Book Company. DO NOT DUPLICATE. 1-888-264-5877.

10. **The fifth paragraph of this passage serves to:**

    F. challenge conventional opinion about political campaigning.

    G. explain why some politicians use negative campaigning.

    H. suggest that candidates cannot stick to the issues.

    J. propose a new way of campaigning.

Copyright © American Book Company. DO NOT DUPLICATE. 1-888-264-5877.

# Chapter 4
# Interpreting Prose Fiction Texts

On the ACT Reading Test, **prose fiction** passages are short stories or excerpts from longer stories or novels. Questions about these passages focus on the same literary elements and devices that you have studied in literature and English classes—plot, characters, theme, mood, and so on.

Within the thirty-five minutes allotted for the ACT Reading Test, you should give yourself an average of eight and a half minutes to read each passage and then answer the ten questions that follow it. Practicing now at your own pace will help you to read passages and answer questions more quickly and accurately when you take the test.

As you read the prose fiction text, pay attention to the elements on the following page. If any of them seem unfamiliar, be sure to review them in literature textbooks or Web sites and work with your teacher or tutor to make sure you understand them.

Copyright © American Book Company. DO NOT DUPLICATE. 1-888-264-5877.

# SPECIAL TRAITS OF PROSE FICTION PASSAGES

| | |
|---|---|
| **Genre** | Literary **genres** are types of literature grouped according to certain conventions and characteristics. Not all works of prose fiction can be included in a genre, but fiction genres include fantasy, romance, western, mystery, science fiction, and others. |
| **Plot** | The **plot** is the sum of events that happens in a story. Every plot has a beginning, middle, and end, usually presented with features such as exposition, rising action, climax, falling action, and resolution, but the structures and timelines of plots vary greatly. Though you will not be asked directly about devices such as flashback, foreshadowing, subplots, conflicts, and so on, remember to look for them, as they affect interpretation of a story. |
| **Mood and Tone** | **Mood** refers to the overall feeling or atmosphere that a piece of literature evokes through diction, setting, and events. For example, the mood of Edgar Allan Poe's "The Tell-Tale Heart" is dark and tense. A writer creates **tone** by conveying attitude and emotion through carefully chosen words. The tone of the main character narrating "The Tell-Tale Heart" is guilt-ridden and paranoid. |
| **Characterization** | Characters that appear in fiction prose are created by the author, though they may be based on real people. **Characterization** is how an author reveals characters to the reader through actions, dialogue, dialect, narration, and description. Remember also the various types of characters such as protagonists, antagonists, foils, archetypes, and static and dynamic characters. Pay special attention to how characters may evolve within a story and how they interact. |
| **Point of View** | An author chooses the most appropriate **point of view** to tell a story. First-person point of view means that one of the characters in the story is recounting the events, which gives the reader that character's perspective. An author using third person point of view usually either focuses on one character's motivations (limited) or reveals the thoughts of many characters (omniscient). |
| **Theme** | **Theme** is the underlying meaning or message conveyed by a literary work. Sometimes a theme can be a message or lesson but often is more subtle, revealing insights into life and human nature rather than teaching. Remember that themes usually are implied. A work often has a central theme, but several themes may be discernible. |

Copyright © American Book Company. DO NOT DUPLICATE. 1-888-264-5877.

As you read in chapter 2, there are some fundamental items that you will want to determine in order to gain general understanding of any passage you read—the **main idea**, **significant details**, **sequence of events**, and any **unfamiliar words or phrases**. In addition, as you read in chapter 3, you also want to read critically to uncover important **comparisons**, **cause-effect relationships**, **generalizations**, and how the author uses **voice and method** to shape a work. This chapter will help you work through how to read passages and answer questions about fiction prose on the ACT Reading Test.

## TYPES OF QUESTIONS YOU WILL SEE

There are two types of questions on the ACT Reading Test:

**Referring** questions ask you about information that is clearly stated in the passage. For instance, a question may ask about a detail that you can readily find expressed in the passage. Try this example.

**Excerpt from passage:** This passage was adapted from "The Dog" by Andrew Barton "Banjo" Paterson, published in 1902.

1    Dogs, like horses, have very keen intuition. They know when the men around them are frightened, though they may not know the cause. In a great Queensland strike, when the shearers attacked and burnt Dagworth shed, some rifle-
5    volleys were exchanged. The air was full of human electricity, each man giving out waves of fear and excitement. Mark now the effect it had on the dogs. They were not in the fighting; nobody fired at them, and nobody spoke to them; but every dog left his master, left the sheep, and went away to the homestead, about six miles
10    off. There wasn't a dog about the shed next day after the fight. The noise of the rifles had not frightened them, because they were well-accustomed to that.

**Which of the following is NOT answered by information in this excerpt?**

**A.** Why did these rifle shots cause the dogs to respond unusually?

**B.** What other animal reacts to the fear of the human beings around it?

**C.** Did the dogs in the Queensland strike try to help their masters?

**D.** To what other human emotions do dogs most noticeably respond?

Copyright © American Book Company. DO NOT DUPLICATE. 1-888-264-5877.

Which answer would you choose? A clue that this is a referring question is the phrase "answered by the information in this passage." This implies that everything you need to choose the correct answer is provided in the passage. For this type of question, a process of elimination can help you find the correct answer: Choice **A** cannot be correct because the paragraph expresses that the dogs responded differently when they sensed fear; **B** is not correct either because the first line states that dogs have this intuition in common with horses; **C** is not correct because the passage mentions the dogs left their masters. **D** is the right answer, as the passage does not mention any other human emotions to which dogs respond. Now, when you take the Reading Test, you will have an entire passage of information from which to pick out facts; however, this example shows you that referring questions are fairly straightforward.

**Reasoning** questions delve deeper by asking you to interpret what you read in the passage. Take a look at a sample reasoning question that could be asked about the same excerpt that you read earlier.

**It is reasonable to infer from this passage that a dog will:**

A. bite its master if it gets too frightened.

B. want to be with other dogs in times of trouble.

C. desire to be near a human who is in a good mood.

D. bring help to its master in the event of danger or alarm.

This question clearly asks you to think beyond what is in the passage. Its wording tells you that you need to make an inference (reasonable assumption) based on what the passage tells you. Now, you must weigh what most reasonably can be assumed based on what the author has written. Considering **A**, the paragraph gave no indication that dogs would turn on their own masters—in fact, the dogs fled—so this inference is not a reasonable one. Choice **B** may be true, but is it the most likely assumption based on the passage? **C** is actually a safer assumption; given that the dogs wanted no part of their masters' fear, it stands to reason that dogs prefer to be around humans who are in good moods. Finally, **D** cannot be correct because we know that the dogs went to their homestead, not to seek help.

When you take the ACT Reading Test, both referring and reasoning questions will follow each passage, and they will be in no particular order. In addition to these two *types* of questions, there will be eight *categories* of questions. As you learned in chapters 2 and 3, most questions will ask you about one or more of the following:

- main ideas
- details
- sequence of events
- words and phrases in context
- comparisons and contrasts
- cause-effect relationships
- generalizations
- author's voice and method

Copyright © American Book Company. DO NOT DUPLICATE. 1-888-264-5877.

Now, take a look at another, longer excerpt from Paterson's story. Following the passage are ten questions that approximate the types and categories of questions you might see after a prose fiction passage on the ACT Reading Test.

**Sample Passage and Questions**

**DIRECTIONS:** After reading the passage, choose the best answer to each question. You may refer to the passage as often as necessary. (Remember, when you take the actual ACT Reading Test, there will be four passages—one of which will be prose fiction—and you will have an answer document on which you will darken ovals corresponding to the questions numbers on the test.)

**PROSE FICTION:** This passage is adapted from the short story "The Dog" by Andrew Barton "Banjo" Paterson. It first appeared in a book of Paterson's short stories entitled *Three Elephant Power and Other Stories*, published in 1917 in Sydney, Australia.

1    The dog is a member of society who likes to have his day's work, and who does it more conscientiously than most human beings. A dog always looks as if he ought to have a pipe in his mouth and a black bag for his lunch, and then he would go quite happily to the office every day.

5    A dog without work is like a man without work, a nuisance to himself and everybody else. People who live about town, and keep a dog to give the children hydatids and to keep the neighbours awake at night, imagine that the animal is fulfilling his destiny. All town dogs, fancy dogs, show dogs, lap-dogs, and other dogs with no work to do, should be abolished; it is only in the country that a dog has any justification for his existence.

10    The old theory that animals have only instinct, not reason, to guide them is knocked endways by the dog. A dog can reason as well as a human being on some subjects, and better on others, and the best reasoning dog of all is the sheepdog. The sheepdog is a professional artist with a pride in his business. Watch any drover's dogs bringing sheep into the yards. How thoroughly they feel their responsibility, and how very annoyed they
15    get if a stray dog with no occupation wants them to stop and fool about! They snap at him and hurry off, as much as to say: "You go about your idleness. Don't you see this is my busy day?"

Sheepdogs are followers of Thomas Carlyle. They hold that the only happiness for a dog in this life is to find his work and to do it. The idle, "dilettante," non-working,
20    aristocratic dog they have no use for.

The training of a sheepdog for his profession begins at a very early age. The first thing is to take him out with his mother and let him see her working. He blunders lightheartedly, frisking along in front of the horse, and his owner tries to ride over him, and generally succeeds. It is amusing to see how that knocks all the gas out of a puppy,
25    and with what a humble air he falls to the rear and glues himself to the horse's heels, scarcely daring to look to the right or to the left, for fear of committing some other breach of etiquette.

Copyright © American Book Company. DO NOT DUPLICATE. 1-888-264-5877.

By degrees, slowly, like any other professional, he learns his business. He learns to bring sheep after a horse simply at a wave of the hand; to force the mob up to a gate where
30 they can be counted or drafted; to follow the scent of lost sheep, and to drive sheep through a town without any master, one dog going on ahead to block the sheep from turning off into by-streets while the other drives them on from the rear.

How do they learn all these things? Dogs for show work are taught painstakingly by men who are skilled in handling them; but, after all, they teach themselves more than the
35 men teach them. It looks as if the acquired knowledge of generations were transmitted from dog to dog. The puppy, descended from a race of sheepdogs, starts with all his faculties directed towards the working of sheep; he is half-educated as soon as he is born. He can no more help working sheep than a born musician can help being musical… It is bred in him. If he can't get sheep to work, he will work a fowl; often and often one can
40 see a collie pup painstakingly and carefully driving a bewildered old hen into a stable, or a stock-yard, or any other enclosed space on which he has fixed his mind. How does he learn to do that? He didn't learn it at all. The knowledge was born with him.

1. **In lines 6 and 7, the author writes, "to give the children *hydatids* and to keep the neighbours awake at night." Considering the context, *hydatids* most likely are:**

   **A.** great love and affection.

   **B.** some type of disease or infection.

   **C.** something fun to play with.

   **D.** nightmares about angry neighbors.

**The best answer is B**. Even if you do not know what hydatids (ringworm infections) are, you can glean the answer from context. The paragraph provides the author's view of things that are annoying about non-working dogs. **A** and **C** are positive and can be ruled out. **D** is also negative, but it seems illogical that a dog could give a child a nightmare about something other than itself. Giving the children ringworm infections and keeping the neighbors awake at night are equally annoying, so **B** works best.

2. **Which of the following statements does NOT describe an attribute that sheep-dogs seem to possess?**

   **F.** They are afraid of horses.

   **G.** They are born to herd.

   **H.** They have a keen sense of smell.

   **J.** They take pride in their work.

**The best answer is F**. The last sentence of the passage supports **G**. The fact that they can "follow the scent of lost sheep" (line 30) supports **H**. And **J** is supported by the third sentence of the third paragraph. Sheepdogs may get run over by horses as puppies, but they continue to work with horses even after learning that it is best to stay behind them.

Copyright © American Book Company. DO NOT DUPLICATE. 1-888-264-5877.

3. **It can be logically inferred from the passage that the author feels that:**

   A. lazy people have lazy dogs.

   B. stray dogs should be trained to work.

   C. all dogs are smarter than people.

   D. unemployed people should be jailed.

**The best answer is A.** This is supported by line 5 states that "A dog without work is like a man without work, a nuisance to himself and everybody else." There is no evidence supporting the information in Choices **B** or **D**. And though the author believes dogs are smarter than some people, he does not say all people, as Choice **C** asserts.

4. **In the first three paragraphs, a working dog is described as being most like:**

   F. a starving artist.

   G. a factory foreman.

   H. a businessperson.

   J. a judge.

**The best answer is H.** Though the dog may be an artist, he's hardly described as a starving one (**F**), which insinuates one who is too lazy to work for his own food. And, though there may be some activities a dog performs that include supervising (**G**) or judging (**J**), the best support is found in lines 3 and 4, "he would go quite happily to the office every day."

5. **According to the passage, a working dog can be most accurately described as:**

   A. arrogant and detached.

   B. content and determined.

   C. carefree and expressive.

   D. fierce and unsociable.

**The best answer is B.** There is no evidence to suggest that the sheepdog is Choice **A**, *detached*, or Choice **D**, *unsociable* (it is very involved in human work), nor is it described as Choice **C**, *carefree* (it is serious and hardworking).

Copyright © American Book Company. DO NOT DUPLICATE. 1-888-264-5877.

6.   **A sheep farmer would most likely agree with which of the following statements about sheepdogs?**

   F.   Sheepdogs are cherished members of the family.

   G.   Sheepdogs are the only animals that earn their keep.

   H.   Sheepdogs have their work to do and do it well.

   J.   Sheepdogs need a great deal of supervision.

**The best answer is H**. Though **F** may be true, it is not mentioned in the passage. The sheepdog is given as an example of the smartest of hardworking dogs, but not the only hardworking animal, as **G** suggests. The last paragraph describes how even an untrained sheepdog can herd animals; it does not need the amount of supervision that **J** suggests.

7.   **The main point of the last paragraph is that:**

   A.   trained sheepdogs can herd any type of animals, not only sheep.

   B.   everything that work dogs do must be carefully taught to them.

   C.   dogs seem to pass knowledge from generation to generation.

   D.   puppies already know everything that they will ever use in their work.

**The best answer is C**. Whether Choice **A** is or isn't a true statement, it would still only be a supporting detail to the main point. The fourth sentence of the paragraph (line 37) states that "he is half-educated as soon as he is born"; this eliminates both **B** and **D**.

8.   **According to the passage, key parts of a sheepdog puppy's training include:**

   I. observe its mother at work.

   II. learn to run behind a horse.

   III. learn to herd chickens.

   F.   II and III only

   G.   I and II only

   H.   I and III only

   J.   I, II, and III

**The best answer is G**. The fifth paragraph supports Roman numerals I and II. Roman numeral III is described in the passage as a possibility for a dog that is untrained, but it is not described as a necessary part of the learning process.

Copyright © American Book Company. DO NOT DUPLICATE. 1-888-264-5877.

9. **According to the passage, we can infer that the cause of Thomas Carlyle's recommendation for happiness was most likely:**

   A. sheep herding.

   B. being a dilettante.

   C. working hard.

   D. keeping sheepdogs.

**The best answer is C**. The fourth paragraph states that "sheepdogs are followers of Thomas Carlyle," meaning they seem to embrace his principles. Even if the reader does not know who Carlyle is, she can infer from the context that Carlyle believed in work. This eliminates **B**. There is no evidence to support **A** or **D**.

10. **What word would best describe the author's tone toward the subject?**

    F. sympathetic

    G. harsh

    H. condescending

    J. admiring

**The best answer is J**. The tone in the first sentence of the passage (lines 1 and 2) shows the author's support of the dog. Here and other places (lines 11 and 12) he touts the dog's superiority to even humans. If the focus of the subject were on humans, **G** or **H** could be correct, but it is not. His focus is on the impressive traits of the dog, specifically the sheepdog, so **G** and **H** are incorrect. He is not really "feeling for" the dog, so **F** is not a possibility.

Copyright © American Book Company. DO NOT DUPLICATE. 1-888-264-5877.

# CHAPTER 4 SUMMARY

**Prose fiction** passages are short stories or excerpts from longer stories or novels.

The **special traits** of prose fiction passages:

- **genre**
- **plot**
- **mood and tone**
- **characterization**
- **point of view**
- **theme**

Copyright © American Book Company. DO NOT DUPLICATE. 1-888-264-5877.

# CHAPTER 4 REVIEW

**PROSE FICTION:** This passage is adapted from the short story "Seeds" by Sherwood Anderson (1861–1946). It appears in an anthology of his work entitled *Triumph of the Egg and Other Stories*.

1    He was a small man with a beard and was very nervous. I remember how the cords of his neck were drawn taut.

For years he had been trying to cure
5   people of illness by the method called psychoanalysis. The idea was the passion of his life. "I came here because I am tired," he said dejectedly. "My body is not tired but something
10  inside me is old and worn-out. I want joy. For a few days or weeks I would like to forget men and women and the influences that make them the sick things they are."

15  There is a note that comes into the human voice by which you may know real weariness. It comes when one has been trying with all his heart and soul to think his way along some difficult
20  road of thought. Of a sudden he finds himself unable to go on. Something within him stops. A tiny explosion takes place. He bursts into words and talks, perhaps foolishly. Little side
25  currents of his nature he didn't know were there run out and get themselves expressed. It is at such times that a man boasts, uses big words, makes a fool of himself in general.

30  And so it was the doctor became shrill. He jumped up from the steps where we had been sitting, talking

and walked about. "You come from the West. You have kept away from people.
35  You have preserved yourself! I haven't—" His voice had indeed become shrill. "I have entered into lives. I have gone beneath the surface of the lives of men and women."

40  I began to sense the depths of his weariness. "We will go swim in the lake," I urged.

"I don't want to swim or do any plodding thing. I want to run and
45  shout," he declared. "For awhile, for a few hours, I want to be like a dead leaf blown by the winds over these hills. I have one desire and one only—to free myself."

50  We walked in a dusty country road. I wanted him to know that I thought I understood, so I put the case in my own way.

When he stopped and stared at me
55  I talked. "You are no more and no better than myself," I declared. "You are a dog that has rolled in offal, and because you are not quite a dog you do not like the smell of your own hide."

60  In turn my voice became shrill. "You blind fool," I cried impatiently. "Men like you are fools. You cannot go along that road. It is given to no man to venture far along the road of lives."

65  I became passionately in earnest. "The illness you pretend to cure is the universal illness," I said. "The thing you want to do cannot be done. Fool— do you expect love to be understood?"

70 We stood in the road and looked at each other. The suggestion of a sneer played about the corners of his mouth. He put a hand on my shoulder and shook me. "How smart we are—how
75 aptly we put things!"

He spat the words out and then turned and walked a little away. "You think you understand, but you don't understand," he cried. "What you say
80 can't be done can be done. You're a liar. You cannot be so definite without missing something vague and fine. You miss the whole point. The lives of people are like young trees in a forest.
85 They are being choked by climbing vines. The vines are old thoughts and beliefs planted by dead men. I am myself covered by crawling creeping vines that choke me."

90 He laughed bitterly. "And that's why I want to run and play," he said. "I want to be a leaf blown by the wind over hills. I want to die and be born again, and I am only a tree covered with vines
95 and slowly dying. I am, you see, weary and want to be made clean. I am an amateur venturing timidly into lives," he concluded. "I am weary and want to be made clean. I am covered by
100 creeping crawling things."

1. **As it is used in line 44, the phrase "do any plodding thing" most nearly means:**

   A. do anything boring.

   B. do anything in the water.

   C. do anything in secret.

   D. do anything slowly.

2. **The main point of the second paragraph is that the doctor:**

   F. has a problem that he wants the narrator to solve.

   G. wishes he had chosen another profession.

   H. is exhausted from listening to other people's problems.

   J. thinks that most people's problems are hopeless.

3. **It can be inferred from the passage that when the doctor notes that the narrator is "from the West" (line 34), he is insinuating that the narrator is from:**

   A. a warmer climate.

   B. a rural area with a small population.

   C. a large costal city.

   D. a less cultured part of the country.

4. **When the doctor states in lines 86 and 87 that "the vines are old thoughts and beliefs planted by dead men," he means that:**

   F. the men died, then they planted vines.

   G. the men planted vines, then the men died.

   H. the men planted vines, then the vines died.

   J. the men planted old vines.

Copyright © American Book Company. DO NOT DUPLICATE. 1-888-264-5877.

5. **How does the narrator feel about psychoanalysis?**

    A. He is strongly opposed to it.

    B. He believes it is a useless practice.

    C. He is fascinated by its effect on the doctor.

    D. He wants to use it on the doctor.

6. **How does the doctor feel about psychoanalysis?**

    I. He believes that it works.

    II. He is fatigued from consuming himself with its implementation.

    III. He has given up on it.

    F. II only

    G. I and II only

    H. II and III only

    J. I, II, and III

7. **In terms of developing the narrative, the third paragraph (lines 15–29) primarily serves to:**

    I. describe the effects of "real weariness."

    II. show what really happened when "the doctor became shrill."

    III. reveal to the reader that the doctor really needs to be a patient.

    A. I only

    B. III only

    C. I and II only

    D. I, II, and III

8. **According to his own words, how is the doctor like a tree?**

    F. He is young.

    G. He is covered with vines.

    H. He is covered with leaves.

    J. He is clean.

9. **According to the passage, why does the doctor want to be like a leaf?**

    A. He wants to be free.

    B. He wants to be old.

    C. He wants to travel.

    D. He wants to go unnoticed.

10. **Why is the doctor, according to the narrator, feeling the way he is?**

    F. It's time for the doctor to retire.

    G. The doctor is involving himself in other people's lives.

    H. The doctor has chosen a profession that is not suited to his skills.

    J. The doctor is not used to the fast-paced life.

Copyright © American Book Company. DO NOT DUPLICATE. 1-888-264-5877.

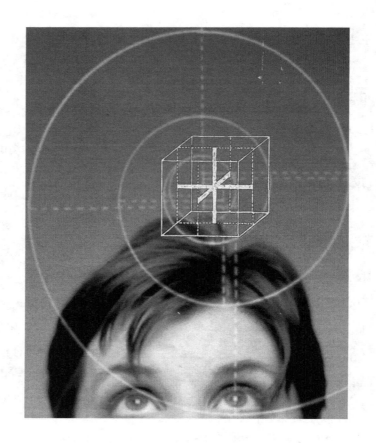

Copyright © American Book Company. DO NOT DUPLICATE. 1-888-264-5877.

# Chapter 5
# Interpreting Humanities Texts

On the ACT Reading Test, **humanities** passages typically explain or examine ideas or works in the areas of architecture, art, dance, ethics, film, language, literary criticism, music, philosophy, radio, television, and theater. These passages are often memoirs or personal essays.

Within the thirty-five minutes allotted for the ACT Reading Test, you should give yourself an average of eight and a half minutes to read each passage and then answer the ten questions that follow it. Practicing now at your own pace will help you to read passages and answer questions more quickly and accurately when you take the test.

As you read the humanities text, pay attention to the elements on the next page. If any of them seem unfamiliar, be sure to review them in literature textbooks or Web sites and work with your teacher or tutor to make sure you understand them.

Copyright © American Book Company. DO NOT DUPLICATE. 1-888-264-5877.

## SPECIAL TRAITS OF HUMANITIES PASSAGES

| | |
|---|---|
| **Exclusively Human Subject** | It shouldn't shock you to learn that humanities writing is all about the experience of being human. Things like philosophy and expressive art provide insight into what it means to be human, and criticism draws further wisdom from these sources by close study. Obviously, natural science passages can analyze humans, but they can also deal with anything from the atom to zebras. Social studies passages certainly are about human behavior, so what's the difference? Well, social studies passages deal with human activities and accomplishments over time; humanities is about how the things these same humans have built, created, written, or composed express the nature of the human spirit. |
| **Cultural Subject** | Humanities is set apart from social studies and science by its focus on aspects of culture, not historical facts or the physical workings of the universe. If a humanities author writes about history, it is usually about something like the history of an architectural period or the political turbulence that inspired a rock band. |
| **Subjective Language** | Similar to prose fiction, humanities passages typically present the author's personal thoughts. However, most humanities passages are less subjective than fiction writing tends to be. Also, unlike traditional science or social studies writing, the humanities author will usually have no problem displaying a **personal bias**. In this regard, you can think of the humanities as a "middle ground," combining traits of both prose fiction and social studies/natural science. This means that you can expect to see questions about author's tone and method. |
| **Frequent Opinions** | Among the three nonfiction passage types, humanities typically involves the largest amount of **author opinion**, since the other two types (science, social studies) are about interpretations of evidence. Questions about humanities passages will usually ask you to use logic rather than track down facts. |
| **Analytical Tone, Intent** | While many social studies and natural science passages are written to analyze information, instead of just deliver facts, humanities passages tend to contain more **analytical writing** than any other kind. In other words, humanities passages depend on argument, while the other kinds of nonfiction passages are more likely to employ evidence and documentation. This won't be as daunting as it all sounds; the book reports you've written since grade school would count as humanities writing, since you wrote them to analyze someone else's work of literature. |

Copyright © American Book Company. DO NOT DUPLICATE. 1-888-264-5877.

As you read in chapter 2, there are some fundamental items that you will want to determine in order to gain general understanding of any passage you read—the **main idea**, **significant details**, **sequence of events**, and any **unfamiliar words or phrases**. In addition, as you read in chapter 3, you also want to read critically to uncover important **comparisons**, **cause-effect relationships**, **generalizations**, and how the author uses **voice and method** to shape a work. This chapter will help you work through how to read passages and answer questions about Humanities on the ACT Reading Test.

# TYPES OF QUESTIONS YOU WILL SEE

Remember, there are two types of questions on the ACT Reading Test:

**Referring** questions ask you about information that is clearly stated in the passage. For instance, a question may ask about a detail that you can readily find expressed in the passage. Read this example.

**Excerpt from passsage:** This passage was adapted from *Recent Tendencies in Ethics* by William Ritchie Sorley, published in 1904.

1    Ethical thought during the last century in England was certainly not without controversy; it was indeed controversial almost to a fault. The controversies of the time centered almost exclusively round two questions: the question of the origin of moral ideas, and the question of the criterion of moral value. These questions were of course
5    traditional in the schools of philosophy; and their controversies defined the traditional opposition of ethical opinion, and separated moralists into two hostile schools known as Utilitarian and Intuitionist.

As regards the origin of moral ideas, the Utilitarian School held that they could be traced to experience. With regard to the criterion or standard of morality, they held that
10    the distinction between right and wrong depended upon the consequences of an action in the way of pleasure and pain. The Intuitionists maintained that moral ideas were in their origin spiritual and had an independent validity; they had a worth and authority for conduct which could not be accounted for by any consequences in which action resulted.

   **What did the Intuitionist school believe about moral ideas?**

   **A.** Morals are spiritual in origin.

   **B.** Morals are traced to experience.

   **C.** Morals depend on pleasure and pain.

   **D.** Morals depend on consequences.

**The best choice is A.** This answer is explicitly stated in lines 11–13 (The Intuitionists maintained that moral ideas were in their origin spiritual and had an independent validity; they had a worth and authority for conduct which could not be accounted for by any consequences in which action resulted). The other three choices are found in the paragraph but not in reference to the question.

Copyright © American Book Company. DO NOT DUPLICATE. 1-888-264-5877.

**Reasoning** questions delve deeper by asking you to interpret what you read in the passage. Take a look at this sample reasoning question about the same excerpt that you read earlier.

**Members of the Utilitarian school would most likely embrace morals based on:**

**A.** the most influential verses from the Bible and Qur'an.

**B.** groundbreaking decisions from historic court cases.

**C.** feelings of guilt or satisfaction upon performing an action.

**D.** works of classical literature like Aesop's fables.

**The best answer is C.** Choice **A** would probably apply better to an Intuitionist who would believe that morals are spiritual things. Similarly, **B** and **D** imply that morals can be based on something besides personal experience, which a Utilitarian would disagree with.

When you take the ACT Reading Test, both referring and reasoning questions will follow each passage, and they will be in no particular order. Remember, in addition to these two *types* of questions, there will be eight *categories* of questions.

- main ideas
- details
- sequence of events
- words and phrases in context
- comparisons and contrasts
- cause-effect relationships
- generalizations
- author's voice and method

Now, take a look at a longer excerpt from a humanities passage. Following the passage are ten questions that approximate the types and categories of questions you might see after a humanities passage on the ACT Reading Test.

Copyright © American Book Company. DO NOT DUPLICATE. 1-888-264-5877.

**Sample Passage and Questions**

**DIRECTIONS:** After reading the passage, choose the best answer to each question. You may refer to the passage as often as necessary.

**HUMANITIES:** This passage is adapted from the Foreword of *Woman as Decoration* written by Emily Burbank. It was originally published in New York in 1917.

1      Having assisted in setting the stage for woman, the next logical step is the consideration of woman herself as an important factor in the decorative scheme of any setting—the vital spark to animate all interior decoration, private or public. The book in hand is intended as a brief guide for the woman who would understand her own type,
5      make the most of it, and know how simple a matter it is to be decorative if she will but master the few rules underlying all successful dressing. As the costuming of woman is an art, the history of that art must be known—to a certain extent—by one who would be an intelligent student of our subject. We have tried to tell the beguiling story of decorative woman, as she appears in frescoes and bas reliefs of Ancient Egypt, on Greek vases, the
10    Gothic woman in tapestry and stained glass, woman in painting, stucco and tapestry of the Renaissance, seventeenth, eighteenth, and nineteenth century woman in portraits.

        Contemporary woman's costume is considered not as fashion but as decorative line and color, a distinct contribution to the interior decoration of her own home or other setting. In this department, woman is given suggestions as to the costuming of herself,
15    beautifully and appropriately, in the ball-room, at the opera, in her boudoir, sun-room or on her shaded porch, in her garden, when driving her own car, by the sea, or on the ice.

        If one would know the story of Woman's evolution and retrogression—that rising and falling tide in civilization—we commend a study of her as she is presented in Art. A knowledge of her costume frequently throws light upon her age; a thorough knowledge
20    of her age will throw light upon her costume.

Copyright © American Book Company. DO NOT DUPLICATE. 1-888-264-5877.

A study of the essentials of any costume, of any period, trains the eye and mind to be expert in planning costumes for every-day use. One learns quickly to discriminate between details which are ornaments, because they have meaning, and those which are only illiterate superfluities, and one learns to master many other points.

25    In the world of caste, costume has gradually evolved until it aims through appropriateness at assisting woman to fulfill her role. With peasants who know only the traditional costume of their province, the task must often be done in spite of the costume, which is picturesque or grotesque, inconvenient, even impossible, but long may it linger to divert the eye! Russia, Germany, France, Spain, Italy, Poland, Scandinavia—all have

30    an endless variety of costumes, rich in souvenirs of folk history and rainbows of color, bizarre in line, but it is costuming the woman of fashion which claims our attention.

Some chapters may, at first glance, seem irrelevant, but those who have seriously studied any art and then undertaken to tell its story briefly in simple, direct language, with the hope of quickly putting audience or reader in touch with the vital links in the

35    chain of evidence, will understand the author's claim that no detour which illustrates the subject can in justice be termed irrelevant. In the detours often lie invaluable data for one with a mind for research—whether author or reader. This is especially true in connection with our present task, which involves unraveling some of the threads from the tangled skein of religion, dancing, music, sculpture, and painting—that mass of bright and

40    somber color, of gold and silver threads, strung with pearls and glittering gems strangely broken by age—which tells the epic-lyric tale of civilization.

The *chic* woman is the one who understands the art of elimination in costumes. Wear your costumes with conviction—by which we mean decide what picture you will make of yourself, make it and then enjoy it! It is only by letting your personality animate your

45    costume that you make yourself superior to the lay figure or the sawdust doll.

**1.**    **As it is used in line 35, the word *detour* most nearly means:**

   **A.** continuance

   **B.** deviation

   **C.** detail

   **D.** chapter

**The best answer is B.** The author is defending chapters that seem to deviate from the basic discussion. **A** is an antonym of *detour*, as it is used here. Choices **C** and **D** fit well enough in the context of the phrase but are not the best answers for the sentence as a whole. Since the author is discussing her own method of seeming to veer off topic, the word *detour* specifically references this in a way that *detail* and *chapter* do not.

Copyright © American Book Company. DO NOT DUPLICATE. 1-888-264-5877.

2.   **One of the main points of the third paragraph (lines 17–20) is that:**

   F.   studying fashion can reveal insights about a woman's life.

   G.   a thorough knowledge of her age will throw light on her costume.

   H.   studying fashion can reveal insights about cultural progression.

   J.   a knowledge of her costume frequently throws light on her era.

**The best answer is H.** Choice **F** misreads the passage; it infers that the author is discussing a single woman when she is really writing about generations of women, using the singular *Woman* the same way other writers have used *Man* to mean *mankind* or *humanity*. Choices **G** and **J** each contain part of the main idea, but Choice **H** sums up both.

3.   **The passage indicates that a *chic* woman is one who:**

   I. wears her costumes with conviction.

   II. understands the art of elimination.

   III. lets her personality animate her costume.

   A.   I only

   B.   II only

   C.   I and III

   D.   II and III

**The best answer is B.** These phrases are all contained in the same paragraph, but only Choice **B** is specifically connected to the idea of a chic woman.

4.   **In terms of developing the passage, the fourth paragraph (lines 21–24) primarily serves to:**

   F.   demonstrate a belief in the power of literacy.

   G.   decry the use of ornaments.

   H.   argue that aesthetics are more important than cultural history.

   J.   show that good fashion requires work and restraint.

**The best answer is J.** In the context of the whole passage, this paragraph emphasizes the need to study in order to succeed. **F** is a misunderstanding on the author's use of *illiterate*; additionally, even if the word were used in the passage to mean "unable to read," this choice would still lack the substance to answer this question. **G** is part of the paragraph's argument but is not the element that contributes the most to the passage. **H** refers to the fifth paragraph and not the fourth.

Copyright © American Book Company. DO NOT DUPLICATE. 1-888-264-5877.

5.  According to the author, the difference between "souvenirs of history and rainbows of color" and "costuming the woman" is that the former is:

    A.  more relevant to this passage than the latter.

    B.  the heart of the whole passage.

    C.  less relevant to this passage than the latter.

    D.  completely irrelevant to the passage.

The best answer is C. Choices A and B confuse the context of this paragraph, while D overstates the disparity between the two. In the fifth paragraph, the author states that some traditional costumes are worn either due to or in spite of their utility, but this is not at issue: this discussion is about fashion.

6.  The sixth paragraph suggests that when the elements of civilization are "untangled" from each other:

    F.  the study of fashion will make more sense.

    G.  a mass of bright, somber color will be strangely broken.

    H.  woman will be free to express herself as she sees fit.

    J.  the epic-lyric tale of civilization will be told.

The best choice is F. Choice G is from a line describing the visual aspects of various fashions. H appears to be more related to the content of a different paragraph. The sentence from the passage that J is based on is about what the "tangle" consists of and not the results of breaking it down.

7.  According to the passage, which art form was popularized after Gothic tapestry and before eighteenth-century art?

    A.  Renaissance stucco

    B.  Ancient Egyptian frescoes

    C.  Greek vases

    D.  nineteenth-century art

The best answer is A. Note that the list of art periods in the first paragraph follows a straightforward sequence. Clues to this include the list's clearly chronological final three items and the fact that the first item features the word "Ancient." Thus, Choices B, C, and D are outside of the range in question.

Copyright © American Book Company. DO NOT DUPLICATE. 1-888-264-5877.

**8. In the second paragraph, the author implies that "woman's costume" was, at one point:**

    **F.** line and color.

    **G.** merely fashion.

    **H.** interior decoration.

    **J.** beautiful and appropriate.

**The best answer is G.** The author's use of the word *contemporary*, which means *modern*, suggests that things are different now than they were in the past. By saying that woman's costume is not thought of as just fashion, the author is implying that it <u>used to be</u> thought of as just fashion. Choice **F** gets this relationship backwards, and Choices **H** and **J** use less relevant terms from the later parts of the paragraph.

**9. Based on what is revealed in this passage, the author would most likely consider a woman dressed in gaudy clothes from a different culture to be:**

    **A.** charming.

    **B.** enlightening.

    **C.** festive.

    **D.** unappealing.

**The best answer is D.** In the fifth paragraph, the author argues that the visual aspects of a garment are far more important than any cultural significance.

**10. According to the passage, a modern, fashionable woman can make herself superior to a doll by:**

    **F.** assisting in setting the stage for other women.

    **G.** learning as much art history as possible.

    **H.** letting her personality shine through her clothes.

    **J.** fulfilling her role according to her social class.

**The best answer is H.** The last paragraph answers this question. Choice **F** refers to something decorative, not to anything directly related to this passage. **G** is offered as advice for fashionable women but in a different context. **J** is from a paragraph on poor people in other cultures, not the book's apparently wealthy target audience.

Copyright © American Book Company. DO NOT DUPLICATE. 1-888-264-5877.

# CHAPTER 5 SUMMARY

**Humanities** passages cover the areas of architecture, art, dance, ethics, film, language, literary criticism, music, philosophy, radio, television, and theater.

The **special traits** of humanities passages:

- **exclusively human content**
- **cultural subject**
- **subjective language**
- **frequent opinions**
- **analytical tone, intent**

# CHAPTER 5 REVIEW

**HUMANITIES:** This passage is adapted from "Radio Panic!" by Dennis Martin (American Book Company © 2008).

1    Before the advent of television, generations of Americans gathered around their radios and listened to music, plays, news reports, and
5    programs. The radio was not just common entertainment; it became the average person's eyes and ears, tuning them into a dynamic and turbulent world, and it had just as much impact
10    on American life as TV and the Internet have on our lives now. However, like all forms of communication, the radio had the power to mislead people.

     Many Americans were already
15    tense in late 1938, hearing nightly news reports about Hitler's tanks and armies swallowing up southeast Europe. To escape from their concerns, many listened to "The Charlie McCarthy
20    Show," the nation's most popular radio program. The stars of the show were Edgar Bergman and his dummy Charlie McCarthy. Competing with this program was the Mercury Group,
25    headed by renegade dramatist Orson Welles. His program, "Mercury Theatre on the Air," aired on another station at the same time as McCarthy's, and Welles was hunting for ways to
30    capture a larger audience. He had the idea of rewriting a well-known novel, *War of the Worlds* by H.G. Wells, and adapting it into a radio play. After many revisions, such as adding many
35    narrators and changing the setting from 1900s England to contemporary New England, Welles felt that the story was invigorated and would be more personal for listeners.

40    Welles aired the play on Mercury Group's Halloween show on October 30, 1938. At eight o'clock that Sunday night, the broadcast began with an announcer saying, "The Columbia
45    Broadcasting System and its affiliated stations present Orson Welles and the *Mercury Theatre on the Air* in *The War*

Copyright © American Book Company. DO NOT DUPLICATE. 1-888-264-5877.

Copyright © American Book Company. DO NOT DUPLICATE. 1-888-264-5877.

*of the Worlds* by H.G. Wells,"
explaining that the radio play was to be
50 presented as if it were regular radio
news, but most listeners began the
evening listening to McCarthy's
program and switched over after
Mercury's notification had been made,
55 thus missing the warning. Even many
of those who heard the Mercury's
acknowledgement that the material was
fiction still mistook the simulated
newscast as an account of real world
60 events. With Nazis on the march in
Europe, an alien invasion of America
was apparently not all that farfetched.
The stage was set for mass hysteria.

As the play began, ordinary dance
65 music was interrupted a number of
times by authentic sounding news
bulletins reporting that a flaming object
had plummeted into a farm near
Grover's Mill, New Jersey. The actors,
70 playing news announcers and
government officials that the public
would expect to hear in a disaster,
described the landing of a mysterious
invasion force. One actor playing a
75 reporter on the scene even details the
emergence of one of the bizarre
creatures from its spacecraft. "Good
heavens, something's wriggling out of
the shadow like a gray snake," he says.
80 "There, I can see the thing's body. The
eyes are black and gleam like a serpent!
The mouth is V-shaped, with saliva
dripping from its rimless lips!"

Further "incoming" news bulletins
85 and broadcasts reported flaming
meteors crashing near Princeton, New
Jersey, killing 1,500 people; later the
meteors were explained as metal
cylinders containing strange beings
90 from Mars armed with gas bombs and
death rays. Because the play was faked

so well, a large portion of the radio
audience thought it was hearing an
actual news account of an attack from
95 Mars, and confusion and panic soon
broke out from Grover's Mill to
Seattle, Washington (after a
coincidental power outage in a nearby
town). People hid in cellars, packed
100 roads, loaded guns, and even wrapped
their heads in wet towels to fend off
deadly Martian gas. Small mobs of
terrified people sought advice on
immediately fleeing New York City.
105 Telephone lines were tied up with
thousands of calls, and sheriff's
departments, newspapers, and the
Associated Press were all scrambling to
separate fact from fiction. People
110 gathered on street corners hoping to
glimpse the sight of a battle in the
skies; in other areas hundreds flocked
to the street and ran in panic. The
switchboard at *The New York Times*
115 was overwhelmed by calls. One man
from Ohio allegedly asked, "What time
will it be the end of the world?"

According to one professor, almost
two million people believed Welles's
120 program was real. Unwittingly or not,
Orson Welles and the Mercury Theatre
made a fascinating and important
demonstration. They proved that well-
made art can convince masses of
125 people of a totally unreasonable
proposition and create widespread
alarm. Dorothy Thompson, writing for
the *New York Tribune*, stated that the
broadcast revealed how politicians
130 could use the power of mass
communication to create theatrical
illusions and manipulate the public.

1. **The word *unwittingly*, as used in line 120, most nearly means:**

    A. deviously.

    B. ignorantly.

    C. benevolently.

    D. accidentally.

2. **According to the passage, Welles's dramatic broadcast was made more convincing by:**

    I. a general sentiment of concern due to war in Europe.

    II. most of the audience missing the opening disclaimer.

    III. its lack of commercial interruptions.

    F. I and II

    G. II and III

    H. I and III

    J. I, II, and III

3. **Which of these correctly presents the passage's sequence of events?**

    A. An announcer warns that the program is fiction, actors playing reporters describe aliens, fake bulletins depict meteors striking a farm, some listeners begin to panic.

    B. Fake bulletins depict meteors striking a farm, actors playing reporters describe aliens, some listeners begin to panic, an announcer warns that the program is fiction.

    C. Fake bulletins depict meteors striking a farm, some listeners begin to panic, actors playing reporters describe aliens, an announcer warns that the program is fiction.

    D. An announcer warns that the program is fiction, fake bulletins depict meteors striking a farm, actors playing reporters describe aliens, some listeners begin to panic.

4. **The main point of this passage is that:**

    F. politicians can use the power of mass communication to manipulate the public.

    G. six million people heard the broadcast, and almost two million believed it was real.

    H. well-made art can convince masses of people of a totally unreasonable proposition.

    J. the radio was not just common entertainment; it was the average person's eyes and ears.

Copyright © American Book Company. DO NOT DUPLICATE. 1-888-264-5877.

5. **Which of the following questions is NOT answered by the information in the passage?**

   A. What event contributed to the panic in Washington state?

   B. How many listeners heard Welles' radio broadcast?

   C. In what year did Hitler's armies invade southeast Europe?

   D. Did Welles change the novel's setting during adaptation?

6. **What is the effect of the author's referencing Dorothy Thompson's *New York Tribune* article?**

   F. to provide background information on radio techniques

   G. to warn the reader of emotional tricks by politicians

   H. to draw humor from Thompson's outdated paranoia

   J. to show the passage's relevance beyond just fiction

7. **Some panicked listeners decided to cover their heads with wet towels, believing this would:**

   A. protect them from poisonous gas.

   B. block the terrifying radio waves.

   C. prevent Martians from spotting them.

   D. become a sign of solidarity among the crowds.

8. **According to the passage, how was radio in the 1930s most similar to today's Internet?**

   F. People believed virtually everything they heard on the radio.

   G. Politicians quickly sought to take advantage of it for propaganda.

   H. It provided information to more Americans than any other medium did.

   J. Popular artists used it, along with special effects, to tell convincing stories.

9. **Based on how he is described in this passage, Orson Welles was:**

   A. committed to telling appealing stories.

   B. angry about Hitler's destructive invasions.

   C. an accomplished science fiction novelist.

   D. the world's best known puppeteer.

10. **It is most reasonable to infer that so many New England listeners called *The New York Times* during the broadcast because:**

    F. Grover's Mill, New Jersey, is only a few dozen miles from New York City.

    G. they believed that a newspaper would have answers to their questions.

    H. the sheriff's departments were all busy dealing with crowd control.

    J. a man from Ohio wanted to know more about the end of the world.

Copyright © American Book Company. DO NOT DUPLICATE. 1-888-264-5877.

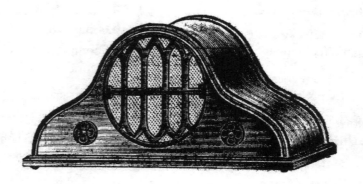

Copyright © American Book Company. DO NOT DUPLICATE. 1-888-264-5877.

# Chapter 6
# Interpreting Social Studies Texts

On the ACT Reading Test, **social studies** passages are in the content areas of anthropology, archaeology, biography, business, economics, education, geography, history, political science, psychology, and sociology.

Within the thirty-five minutes allotted for the ACT Reading Test, you should give yourself an average of eight and a half minutes to read each passage and then answer the ten questions that follow it. Practicing now at your own pace will help you to read passages and answer questions more quickly and accurately when you take the test.

As you read the social studies text, pay attention to the special traits on the next page. If any of them seem unfamiliar, be sure to review them in social studies textbooks or Web sites and work with your teacher or tutor to make sure you understand them.

Copyright © American Book Company. DO NOT DUPLICATE. 1-888-264-5877.

## SPECIAL TRAITS OF SOCIAL STUDIES PASSAGES

| | |
|---|---|
| **The Study of Human Behavior** | Social studies is an attempt to explain which person or group of people did what things and why/when/where/how they did them (and, maybe, whether they are likely to do them again). As you read social studies passages, you'll see some personal interpretations by authors, but most will tend to draw from things that can be proved. Questions about social studies passages will likewise put both sides of your brain to work. |
| **Mostly Formal Language** | The language of most social studies passages falls somewhere between the styles used in humanities and natural science authors, as far as formality goes. Writers of natural sciences passages typically use **formal language** and avoid poetic techniques, but humanities authors can be as dramatic and colorful as their subjects. Social studies passages will feature a combination of the two; a passage about a very large war, for instance, may use both metaphors and statistics to express widespread devastation. For these passages, you'll need to be comfortable with both formal and informal language. |
| **Some Bias** | The kind of slant that may affect social studies authors is different from that of writers of humanities passages. While humanities writers display **biased opinions** proudly, social studies writers try to avoid subjectivity. However, keep an eye out for some bias when reading social studies passages, since the issues being discussed are often inflammatory to at least one group of people (whether along racial, religious, national, or political lines). For this reason, when answering test questions, remember that you are only answering according to the passage and not according to what you may know or believe about the topic. |
| **Analysis of Facts** | While natural sciences passages document ideas and humanities passages analyze human creations, social studies passages can both **investigate facts** and interpret them. Economists, for example, use mathematical data based on choices made by members of large groups of people (scientifically processing statistical data), but they then interpret their findings according to their own opinions (similar to the work of those who study humanities). |

Copyright © American Book Company. DO NOT DUPLICATE. 1-888-264-5877.

As you read in chapter 2, there are some fundamental items that you will want to determine in order to gain general understanding of any passage you read—the **main idea**, **significant details**, **sequence of events**, and any **unfamiliar words or phrases**. In addition, as you read in chapter 3, you also want to read critically to uncover important **comparisons**, **cause-effect relationships**, **generalizations**, and how the author uses **voice and method** to shape a work. This chapter will help you work through how to read passages and answer questions about Social Studies on the ACT Reading Test.

## TYPES OF QUESTIONS YOU WILL SEE

There are two types of questions on the ACT Reading Test:

**Referring** questions ask you about information that is clearly stated in the passage. For instance, a question may ask about a detail that you can readily find expressed in the passage. Try this example.

**Excerpt from passage:** Adapted from *Social Life at Rome in the Age of Cicero* by W. Warde Fowler, published in 1909.

1    The baking trade must have given employment to a large number of persons. So did the supply of vegetables, which were brought into the city from gardens outside, and formed, after the corn, the staple food of the lower classes.
5    The ancients were fully alive to the value of vegetable food and of fruit as a healthy diet in warm climates. The very names of some Roman families, like the Fabii and Caepiones, carry us back to a time when beans and onions, which later on were not so much in favour, were a regular
10    part of the diet of the Roman people. The list of vegetables and herbs which we know of as consumed fills a whole page in Marquardt's interesting account of this subject, and includes most of those which we use at the present day.

      It was only when the consumption of meat and game came in with the growth of
15    capital and its attendant luxury that a vegetarian diet came to be at all despised. This is another result of the economic changes caused by the Hannibalic war, and is curiously illustrated by the speech of the cook of a great household in the *Pseudolus* of Plautus, who prides himself on not being as other cooks are, who make the guests into beasts of the field, stuffing them with all kinds of food which cattle eat and even with things which
20    cattle would refuse!

**According to the passage, what was the staple food of the lower classes?**
   **A.** fruit          **B.** corn          **C.** herbs          **D.** meat
Lines 2–3 state that "vegetables… formed, *after* the corn, the staple food of the lower classes," so **the best answer is B**.

Copyright © American Book Company. DO NOT DUPLICATE. 1-888-264-5877.

**Reasoning** questions delve deeper by asking you to interpret what you read in the passage. Take a look at a sample reasoning question, using the same excerpt that you read earlier.

**We can infer from the passage that the "economic changes caused by the Hannibalic war":**

   I. helped the Roman economy grow.

   II. decreased the widespread consumption of vegetables.

   III. were documented in the *Pseudolus* of Plautus.

   **A.** I only

   **B.** I and II only

   **C.** III only

   **D.** II and III only

**The best answer is B.** The Hannibalic war is associated with the "growth of capital" in the second paragraph, which means Roman numeral I is true; this makes **A** and **B** possible correct answers. This paragraph also states that the "vegetarian diet came to be…despised" at this time, which supports Roman numeral II. Aside from the fact that Roman numeral III would be a referring answer to a reasoning question, there is no evidence to show the Hannibalic war was documented in the *Pseudolus*, so neither **C** nor **D** can be correct.

When you take the ACT Reading Test, both referring and reasoning questions will follow each passage, and they will be in no particular order. In addition to these two *types* of questions, there will be eight *categories* of questions. As you learned in chapters 2 and 3, most questions will ask you about one or more of the following:

- main ideas
- details
- sequence of events
- words and phrases in context
- comparisons and contrasts
- cause-effect relationships
- generalizations
- author's voice and method

Now, take a look at a longer passage. Following the passage are ten questions that approximate the types and categories of questions you might see after a social studies passage on the ACT Reading Test.

Copyright © American Book Company. DO NOT DUPLICATE. 1-888-264-5877.

## Sample Passage and Questions

**DIRECTIONS:** After reading the passage, choose the best answer to each question. You may refer to the passage as often as necessary.

**SOCIAL SCIENCE:** This passage is adapted from "War Spreads West" (American Book Company ©2008).

1     Though not as popular among history enthusiasts as its "sequel" in the 1940s, the First World War, ironically known as The War to End All Wars, had about as much impact on modern civilization, influencing events from the rise of Adolf Hitler to the current array of turmoil in the Middle East. The war began on June 28, 1914, when an obscure

5  Austrian noble, Archduke Francis Ferdinand (heir to the throne of Austria-Hungary), was visiting Sarajevo, the capital of his empire's province of Bosnia. Gavrilo Princip, a member of a Yugoslav nationalist group that wanted to take Bosnia from the empire, shot the Archduke during a parade gone awry.

    Austria-Hungary accused its neighbor, Serbia, of plotting to kill the Archduke and

10  threatened to attack. Russia, long allied with Serbia, promised to retaliate against Austria-Hungary. Germany had agreed before the war to support Austria-Hungary, and France kept its word with Russia and mobilized its forces to tie up German armies. Within two months, most Europeans were either directly involved in the war, whether as victims or participants, or worried about the spreading conflict. While beginning a grueling war with

15  Russia in Eastern Europe, Germany decided to flood troops through neutral Belgium in time to cripple France's war effort. The British Empire had promised Belgium it would enter the war if Germany followed this plan. Germany did, and Britain joined France and Russia, forming the loose alliance called the Entente Powers (Triple Entente). Several small or distant nations refused to fight, but Spain was the only major European nation to

20  avoid participating in the war.

    Germany entered France, coming within visual range of Paris's Eiffel Tower until the French stopped their advance at the hideous and costly First Battle of the Marne. For the next wave, the French dug trenches as defensive positions, a technique theorized sixty years earlier but never put into common practice. The Germans did the same, and soon

25  lines of opposing trenches stretched from Switzerland to the North Sea, long gashes in the earth teeming with men, equipment, decay, and disease. Over the next three years the opposing armies hunkered down, digging in and constantly fortifying their trenches. In between lay the notorious "No Man's Land"—a stretch of blighted soil strewn with landmines, barbed wire, and deadly booby traps.

30     When each side began using machine guns and poison gas, the war turned especially hellish. Firing bullets with unprecedented speed, two soldiers operating a machine gun were able to shoot as many rounds as eighty soldiers armed with ordinary rifles. Artillery canisters of deadly gas, from the chlorine clouds first used by the French to the mustard gas developed by the Germans, killed or disabled soldiers instantly. As the artillery

35  exploded, gas engulfed the soldiers, liquefying their internal organs and leaving them struggling for breath. Often, gas destroyed the soldiers' lungs, causing them to fill with fluid, literally drowning them from the inside out. The Germans launched over sixty

thousand tons of gas during the war, bringing swift condemnation from the Entente who, of course, also launched about sixty thousand tons. Trench warfare, combined with brutal
40 new technology and consistently terrible leadership, led to the deaths of millions.

Another important development in the war was the first ever wartime use of aircraft. At the beginning of the war, nations used planes primarily for scouting and reconnaissance. Throughout the war, hundreds of competing airplane designs were rushed into production. By the end of the conflict in 1918, countries equipped airplanes with
45 propellers timed to allow pilots to fire machine guns and attack enemy aircraft, and both sides had developed bomber aircraft strong enough to fly deep into enemy territory and drop explosives on towns or factories.

From the war's outset, most of the people of the United States argued for neutrality. President Woodrow Wilson—who ran for reelection in 1916 on the slogan "He Kept Us
50 Out of War"—urged Americans to resist the constant propaganda coming from Germany and the Allied nations. However, various economic factors pushed Wilson toward declaring war against Germany. For example, numerous business interests were tied to Great Britain, as it supplied the nation with weapons and other supplies. Production corporations were eager for a war effort because they knew the military would purchase
55 huge amounts of equipment. With a war, employment and productivity would increase. Moreover, wealthy bankers such as J. P. Morgan had loaned millions of dollars to Great Britain as it fought Germany. The banking elite had a stake in seeing Great Britain win the war and repay its loans with interest. Still, the United States watched the war from a distance until a German submarine sank the American-laden ship *Lusitania* in May 1917,
60 when Wilson was able to convince the nation to plunge into the fray.

1. **Which of the following actions did both Germany and the Entente Powers take?**

    I. launching thousands of tons of poison gas

    II. guarding trenches with machine guns

    III. sending bombers deep into enemy territory

    **A.** I and II

    **B.** II and III

    **C.** I and III

    **D.** I, II, and III

**The best answer is D.** The fourth and fifth paragraphs indicate that both sides used all three of these tactics.

Copyright © American Book Company. DO NOT DUPLICATE. 1-888-264-5877.

2.  **Which of the following questions is NOT answered by the passage?**

    F.  Would the United States have entered the war if not for the *Lusitania* incident?

    G.  Which nation was the first to use both chemical and trench warfare?

    H.  By what method did Gavrilo Princip kill Francis Ferdinand?

    J.  Did Germany face detrimental consequences for its decision to invade Belgium?

**The best answer is F.** The passage implies that the incident was what convinced President Wilson to call for war. Choice **G** is ruled out in line 23 (line containing "the French dug trenches as defensive positions") and 33 (line containing "from the chlorine clouds first used by the French"). Line 5 states that Princip shot Ferdinand, so **H** is incorrect, and **J** is also incorrect since lines 16–17 suggest the consequences were severe.

3.  **The word *blighted*, as it is used in line 28, most nearly means:**

    A.  tilled and irrigated.

    B.  undeveloped.

    C.  cursed.

    D.  ruined.

**The best answer is D.** Much of the land was certainly used for agriculture before the war, but no farms would be able to function among land mines, poison gas, and two massive armies, so Choice **A** is incorrect. **B** and **C** are closer to being correct; however, **B** is vague and fails to suggest destruction, and **C** is different in tone from the rest of the passage, which tends to avoid poetic hyperbole.

4.  **One of the main points of the second paragraph (lines 9–20) is that:**

    F.  major European leaders were eager to fight a war for economic reasons.

    G.  major European nations quickly joined the war.

    H.  major European leaders were eager to fight a war for nationalist reasons.

    J.  major European nations desperately avoided the war.

**The best answer is G.** The paragraph does not attempt to imply any particular motives held by European leaders, so Choices **F** and **H** are not supported. **J** is also incorrect due to the last sentence in the paragraph: "Spain was the only major European nation to avoid participating in the war."

Copyright © American Book Company. DO NOT DUPLICATE. 1-888-264-5877.

5.  **According to the passage, every innovation made by either side caused its opponents to:**

    A. lose hope and attempt to retreat.

    B. employ something equally deadly.

    C. come up with something even more deadly.

    D. plead for the United States to enter the war.

**The best answer is C.** According to the third and fourth paragraphs, the Germans and French were constantly one-upping each other; the fifth paragraph suggests other nations also joined race to utilize increasingly destructive weapons. There is no significant evidence in the passage for Choices **A**, **B**, or **D**.

6.  **According to the passage, certain American bankers and corporations wanted their country to participate in fighting because they:**

    F. knew their companies could make a lot of money off of the war.

    G. were terrified of the German navy crossing the Atlantic Ocean.

    H. wanted to see the liberation of France and Belgium.

    J. were eager to trade freely with nations like Switzerland and Sweden.

**The best answer is F.** The final paragraph supports this choice. The remaining three answer choices are not supported in the passage.

7.  **According to the passage, what did the Austro-Hungarian Empire and Princip's nationalist group have in common?**

    A. location in western Europe

    B. desire to directly govern Bosnia

    C. urge to start war between Russia and Germany

    D. attempts to develop chemical weapons

**The best answer is B.** The first paragraph explains how the group Princip belonged to wanted Austria-Hungary to leave Bosnia. **A** is incorrect, since the passage makes no mention of these parties being in Western Europe; in fact, they were both in Eastern Europe. **C** is also false; whatever Princip's intentions may have been, starting a massive war is not mentioned in the passage as one of them. There is also no indication in the passage of either of these groups using chemical weapons, so **D** is incorrect.

Copyright © American Book Company. DO NOT DUPLICATE. 1-888-264-5877.

**8. The passage implies that trench warfare:**

 I. was effective at stopping enemy advances.

 II. cost the lives of many soldiers.

 III. made aircraft necessary tools of war.

 **F.** I and II only

 **G.** II and III only

 **H.** I and III only

 **J.** I, II, and III

**The best answer is F.** The passage implies that both sides were able to prevent enemy advances by remaining "hunkered down" for "the next three years." Trench warfare is also listed, at the end of the fourth paragraph, as one of the most deadly elements of the war. The monotony of trench warfare may have inspired commanders to experiment more with aircraft, but there is no evidence in the passage of this.

**9. Based on this passage, which of these is the best description of Gavrilo Princip's impact on history?**

 **A.** He brilliantly plotted to start one of the biggest wars ever, knowing that Austria-Hungary would lose once the United States joined, and Bosnia would be free.

 **B.** He provided the spark that caused most European nations to follow each other into a horrific battle, greatly altering world history from 1914 to the present.

 **C.** He was a coward who was in the right place at the right time.

 **D.** He was shot to death by Francis Ferdinand, leaving his empire no choice but to accuse Serbia of involvement in his assassination.

**The best answer is B.** It is evident from the second paragraph that most of these nations were ready for war, having secured alliances and battle plans (such as Britain promising to attack once Germany invaded Belgium and the French having "theorized" strategies "sixty years earlier") with each other before fighting even began. Still, it took Princip's action to give them all a pretext. Choice **A** overstates his motives and foresight; Princip only attempted to escalate the conflict between his group and one nation. **C** is incorrect; no matter how much we may disapprove of assassination, it's hard to call someone a coward for publicly shooting a royal heir. Also, Princip's group membership suggests that he was not just "in the right place at the right time," but given orders to be there. Choice **D** confuses Princip and Ferdinand.

Copyright © American Book Company. DO NOT DUPLICATE. 1-888-264-5877.

10. **Based on the Germans having come "within visual range of Paris's Eiffel Tower," how far did they advance into France?**

    F.  beyond Paris

    G.  to the middle of the city

    H.  They had conquered France.

    J.  a few miles from Paris

**The best choice is J.** Visual range implies that they were only close enough to see the thousand-foot tower, not that they were close enough to claim it. The three other choices are therefore exaggerations.

---

## CHAPTER 6 SUMMARY

**Social studies** passages are in the content areas of anthropology, archaeology, biography, business, economics, education, geography, history, political science, psychology, and sociology.

The **special traits** of social studies passages:

- **the study of human behavior**
- **mostly formal language**
- **some bias**
- **analysis of facts**

Copyright © American Book Company. DO NOT DUPLICATE. 1-888-264-5877.

# CHAPTER 6 REVIEW

**SOCIAL SCIENCE:** This passage is adapted from *Applied Psychology for Nurses* by Mary F. Porter, published in 1921.

1      No mind retains consciously everything that has ever impressed it. It is necessary that it put aside what ceases to be of importance or value and
5   make way for new impressions. We found early in our study that the subconscious never forgets but harbors the apparently forgotten throughout the years, allowing it to modify our
10   thinking, our reactions. But the conscious mind cannot be cluttered with the things of little importance when the more essential is clamoring. So there is a forgetting that is very
15   normal. We forget numberless incidents of our childhood and youth; we may forget the details of much that we have learned to do automatically; but the subconscious mind is attending
20   to them for us.

We forget details we have entrusted to others as not a part of our responsibility. We forget the things which in no way concern us, in which
25   we have no interest, and about which we have no curiosity. And it is well that we do so. If it were not for the ability to forget, our minds would be like a room in which we have lived a lifetime,
30   where we have left everything that has been brought into it since our birth. It would be piled ceiling high, with no room for us, and only with difficulty could we find what we want.

35      But what of the things we must use frequently and cannot find in our minds? What of absent-mindedness and faulty memory? In such cases our minds might be compared to a cluttered
40   room full of things we need and want to use every day, but in confusion. We know where many of them are, the ones we care most about; but we have to rummage wildly to find the rest. We
45   have no proper system of arrangement of our belongings. You laid down that book somewhere, absent-mindedly, and now you cannot tell where. You were thinking of something else at the
50   time, and inattention proves a most common cause of poor memory. Perhaps you simply have more books than the room can hold in an orderly way, and so you crowded that one in
55   some corner, and now have no recollection of where you put it.

Poor memory is the result of lack of attention, or divided attention at the time the particular attention-stimulus
60   knocked. You asked me to buy a ribbon of a certain shade and a certain width when I went to town. I was thinking of my dentist appointment. However, I heard your request, answered it
65   graciously, took the money you offered, still wondering if the dentist would have to draw that tooth. And the chances are that I forgot your ribbon. I was giving you only a passive and
70   divided attention.

Hence we find that a faulty memory may exist in an otherwise normal mind when poor attention, or divided attention due to emotional
75   stress or to an overcrowded mind, which makes it impossible to properly assort its material, interferes.

Again, we forget many things because they are unpleasant to
80   remember. We have no desire, no emotional stimulus to make us remember; or because some of the associations with the forgotten

Copyright © American Book Company. DO NOT DUPLICATE. 1-888-264-5877.

85 incident are undesirable. We forget many things because if we remembered them we would feel called upon to do some unpleasant duty.

90 Thus a forgetting may be purely the result of an emotional interference which makes it, all in all, more pleasant to forget than to remember. If we would help ourselves or our patients whose memories are faulty, and who make them worse by their continual fretting over their disability, we must train
95 ourselves to be willing to forget all that does not in the least concern our interests or those of the people about us, and does not add anything desirable to our knowledge. Thus we may avoid
100 overcrowding the mind. But when we would remember, let us give our whole active attention at the moment of presentation of the new stimulus and immediately tie it up with something in
105 past experience; let us recognize what it is that we should remember and call the reinforcement of will, which demands that we remember whether we want to or not. Sincere desire to
110 remember will inspire early and frequent recalling, with various associations, or hooks, until the impression becomes permanent.

The average patient's poor memory
115 is made worse by his agitation and attention to it, and his conviction that he cannot remember. The fear of forgetting often wastes mental energy which might otherwise provide
120 keenness of memory. If the nurse ties up some pleasant association with the things she wants the sick man to remember, and disregards his painful effort to recall other things, then—
125 unless the mind is disordered—he will often find normal memory reasserting itself.

1. **As it is used in line 67, the word *draw* most nearly means:**

   A. to frame or formulate.

   B. to cause to move in a particular direction.

   C. to sketch.

   D. to extract.

2. **Which of the following statements is the main idea of the first paragraph (lines 1–20)?**

   F. The subconscious never forgets.

   G. There is a forgetting that is very normal.

   H. The subconscious modifies our thinking.

   J. We forget numberless incidents of our childhood and youth.

3. **Which of the following is NOT a cause of poor memory stated in the passage?**

   A. lack of attention

   B. poor physical health

   C. lack of desire to remember

   D. divided attention

4. **In the fourth paragraph, the narrator gives an example of divided attention. In this example, what causes her to forget to buy the ribbon?**

   F. She doesn't really seem interested in buying the ribbon.

   G. She is thinking about a book that she lost earlier that day.

   H. She's concerned with what may happen at the dentist office.

   J. She intends to keep the money instead of buying the ribbon.

Copyright © American Book Company. DO NOT DUPLICATE. 1-888-264-5877.

5. **The author uses an analogy of a room twice—once in the second paragraph and once in the third. Which of these statements accurately compares these two rooms?**

   I. The room in paragraph two is a mind that forgets nothing; the room in paragraph three is a mind with faulty memory.

   II. In both rooms, it is difficult to find things.

   III. The room in paragraph three is more crowded than the room in paragraph two.

   A. I only

   B. III only

   C. I and II only

   D. I, II, and III

6. **According to the passage, the average patient's poor memory is made worse by all of the following EXCEPT:**

   F. being distracted by those trying to help.

   G. being convinced that he cannot remember.

   H. being fearful of forgetting.

   J. being agitated about his poor memory.

7. **According to the passage, what is a cause of divided attention?**

   A. sickness

   B. emotional stress

   C. genetic abnormalities

   D. overexcitement

8. **According to the passage, all of the following could cause a person to forget an incident EXCEPT:**

   F. undesirable mental associations with the memory.

   G. the lack of memorable emotional stimulus.

   H. having no desire to remember the incident.

   J. the incident having occurred too long ago.

9. **According to the passage, a nurse can help a patient with his memory by:**

   I. training herself to be willing to forget things that are not important.

   II. disregarding the patient's painful effort to recall other things.

   III. creating a pleasant association with things the patient needs to remember.

   A. I only

   B. I and II only

   C. II and III only

   D. I, II, and III

10. **According to the passage, the subconscious:**

   F. constantly forgets more things.

   G. forgets only when necessary.

   H. rarely forgets.

   J. never forgets.

Copyright © American Book Company. DO NOT DUPLICATE. 1-888-264-5877.

Copyright © American Book Company. DO NOT DUPLICATE. 1-888-264-5877.

# Chapter 7
# Interpreting Natural Sciences Texts

On the ACT Reading Test, **natural sciences** passages can focus on the content areas of anatomy, astronomy, biology, botany, chemistry, ecology, geology, medicine, meteorology, microbiology, natural history, physiology, physics, technology, or zoology.

Within the thirty-five minutes allotted for the ACT Reading Test, you should give yourself an average of eight and a half minutes to read each passage and then answer the ten questions that follow it. Practicing now at your own pace will help you read passages and answer questions more quickly and accurately when you take the test.

As you read a natural sciences text, pay extra attention to any unfamiliar theories and laws. If a concept or piece of information seems new to you, be sure to clarify it by using science textbooks and Web sites or by working with your teacher or tutor.

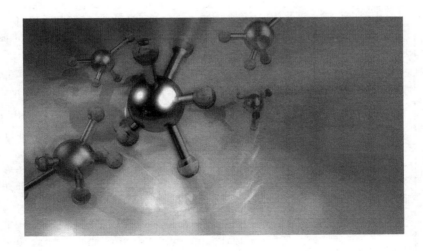

Copyright © American Book Company. DO NOT DUPLICATE. 1-888-264-5877.

# SPECIAL TRAITS OF NATURAL SCIENCES PASSAGES

| Various Subjects | While natural sciences passages can be about things like the chemical composition of the human body or the evolution of humanity, they are more likely to be about subjects besides humans. Anything in the universe that can be theorized about, observed, or tested can be part of the natural sciences. |
|---|---|
| Scientific Method | You've probably read about observation, experimentation, and hypothesis in a science class before. Both natural sciences and social studies passages use the scientific method, but natural sciences passages rely on it almost exclusively. |
| Formal Language | Almost all natural sciences passages avoid informal language. Some even use math. Instead of metaphors, authors may use detailed analogies with every step explained. To answer natural sciences passages, you should practice processing formal language. |
| Lack of Bias | Personal opinion in natural sciences writing is usually unacceptable. When something is unknown, natural sciences authors predict and guess based on whatever evidence is available, but good scientists treasure facts and have little interest in personal opinions. |
| Point of View | An author chooses the most appropriate **point of view** to tell a story. First-person point of view means that one of the characters in the story is recounting the events, which gives the reader that character's perspective. An author using third person point of view usually either focuses on one character's motivations (limited) or reveals the thoughts of many characters (omniscient). |
| Theme | **Theme** is the underlying meaning or message conveyed by a literary work. Sometimes a theme can be a message or lesson but often is more subtle, revealing insights into life and human nature rather than teaching. Remember that themes usually are implied. A work often has a central theme, but several themes may be discernible. |
| Straightforward | While fiction writers rarely state exactly what their stories mean, and humanities and social studies authors can seem evasive at times about arguments, natural sciences writers know that their passages are pointless if they don't get right to the heart of the issue. When reading a test passage, remember that all well-written natural sciences passages will present everything the reader needs to know about the topic. Knowing this, you can focus on understanding the causal and comparative relationships, the sequencing, and the specialized vocabulary within the passage. |

Copyright © American Book Company. DO NOT DUPLICATE. 1-888-264-5877.

## TYPES OF QUESTIONS YOU WILL SEE

There are two types of questions on the ACT Reading Test:

**Referring** questions ask you about information that is clearly stated in the passage. For instance, a question may ask about a detail that you can readily find expressed in the passage. Read this example.

**Natural Science:** Many doctors and scientists agree that medical management based on individual patient genetics and lifestyles is the wave of the future and the key to breakthroughs in effective healthcare.

**This passage states that, to be increasingly effective, medical care should move toward:**

**A.** using data from recent genome research.

**B.** involving only doctors most familiar with the patient.

**C.** basing treatment on individual patient information.

**D.** making major breakthroughs rather than managing individuals' health.

Which answer would you choose? As you can see, there is a clue that this is a referring question in the wording, "This passage states." It means that the answer you are seeking is given to you in the passage. Knowing that, you need to find it and determine which of the answer choices best approximates it. Here, **the best answer is C**, since it is another way of saying what the excerpt says. The other choices are not good matches. Of course, when you take the Reading Test, passages won't be just one sentence long—you'll seek out facts from an entire passage for groups of questions.

**Reasoning** questions delve deeper by asking you to interpret what you read in the passage. Take a look at a sample reasoning question that could be asked about the same excerpt you read earlier.

**Excerpt from passage:** Many doctors and scientists agree that medical management based on individual patient genetics and lifestyles is the wave of the future and the key to breakthroughs in effective healthcare.

**Based on this passage, the author would most agree with which of the following statements?**

**A.** Health care is not well-managed and, therefore, has become excessively expensive.

**B.** Researchers need to conduct further studies about how lifestyle affects health.

**C.** The future of traditional medicine lies in education rather than treatment.

**D.** Physicians need to take more time in interviewing and examining patients.

Copyright © American Book Company. DO NOT DUPLICATE. 1-888-264-5877.

Let's first examine the incorrect answers. Choice **A** mentions the expense of healthcare, which is not discussed in the passage. Any time an answer choice includes information that is not contained or referred to in the passage, it is an incorrect answer. This principle can also be used to eliminate **C** because education is not mentioned in the passage. The passage focuses on the many doctors and scientists, which would include researchers, who agree on the subject of lifestyle as it relates to healthcare; it does not support **B**. In order to be knowledgeable of a patient's genetics and lifestyle, a doctor would need to take more time in interviewing and examining patients. **The best answer is D.**

When you take the ACT Reading Test, both referring and reasoning questions will follow each passage, and they will be in no particular order. In addition to these two *types* of questions, there will be eight *categories* of questions. As you learned in chapters 2 and 3, most questions will ask you about one or more of the following:

- main ideas
- details
- sequence of events
- words and phrases in context
- comparisons and contrasts
- cause-effect relationships
- generalizations
- author's voice and method

Now, let's take a look at a longer natural sciences passage. Following the passage are ten questions that approximate the types and categories of questions you might see after a natural sciences passage on the ACT Reading Test.

**Sample Passage and Questions**

**DIRECTIONS:** After reading the passage, choose the best answer to each question. You may refer to the passage as often as necessary.

**NATURAL SCIENCE:** This passage is adapted from "The Life Cycle of Stars" (©2008 American Book Company).

1    Though no one has ever been able to observe the full life of a star, the universe has provided so many examples of stars at various stages that astronomers have been able to piece together the basics of the stellar life cycle. The first step occurs when space gases, plasma, and dust collect into massive clouds called nebulae. Though a nebula contains

5    helium and assorted other elements, its contents are ninety-seven percent hydrogen. Nebulae have regions of varying density within them, and when regions become dense enough, their gravitational forces cause gases to pool. This accretion process continues until larger and much denser structures, called protostars, begin to form.

       Increased density, pressure, and heat prevent a protostar from completely collapsing

10   under its own gravity. Protostars can range in color from bright blue to deep red, but most

Copyright © American Book Company. DO NOT DUPLICATE. 1-888-264-5877.

are a fiery orange, even though they all appear to the naked eye as white. A critical temperature must be reached for nuclear fusion to begin within a protostar.

Once fusion begins, the protostar matures into a main sequence star. It is at this stage in the star's life when radiation is emitted from its core to its surface. The main sequence
15   stage makes up ninety percent of a normal star's lifetime. Our sun is at this stage. Throughout the main sequence stage, the star contracts as hydrogen is converted to helium through nuclear fusion. This conversion increases the pressure and temperature of its core. As a result, the composition of the star changes, which increases its luminosity and alters its color. Though our sun is not a large star, it is especially luminous when compared with
20   nearby stars, which are mostly older.

Once a star's core hydrogen is totally converted to helium, gravitational forces collapse the core further, and rapid heating causes the outer layers of the star to expand. This continues until the core begins to form iron, marking the end of the fusion process. Eventually, the outer layers cool and the color of the star shifts from its normal color to
25   reddish tones. At this stage, the star has become a red giant. When our sun becomes a red giant in about five billion years, it will be large enough to envelop the orbit of Mars.

Toward the final stages of a star's life, its fate depends on its size. Some tiny stars will outlive our sun by trillions of years, while hypergiant stars may only survive for ten million. Most stars, like our sun, follow the typical pattern. As the core of a normal star
30   becomes more compact, its outer layers, containing heavier elements such as carbon and silicon, are ejected. This forms a planetary nebula. If the core is less than 1.4 times as massive as the sun, the remnant is called a white dwarf and cools into a black dwarf after about one trillion years. Our sun will become a white dwarf in about seven billion years. If, however, the solar mass of the core is larger than 1.4, the gravitation forces become so
35   strong that the core can no longer support its own mass. Even atoms collapse under this pressure. When this happens, energy is released as a colossal shockwave; this explosion is called a supernova.

The energy from a supernova produces light and accelerates the star's matter to one-tenth the speed of light, spreading matter through nearby space in a fantastic display.
40   Larger core remnants sometimes generate a black hole. A supernova's extra materials construct objects like asteroids, moons, and planets, which will remain subject to the developing star's gravity.

The death of a star is not necessarily its end. Existence in distant space is subject to natural cycles of death and birth, just as it is on our planet. If the particles discharged by
45   a supernova do not form a black hole, they can instead collect into a new nebula that will, in turn, give way to a new star. From nebula to nebula, the process can take anywhere from millions to trillions of years to complete.

Copyright © American Book Company. DO NOT DUPLICATE. 1-888-264-5877.

1. **As it is used in line 7, *accretion* most nearly means:**
   A. accumulation.

   B. actualization.

   C. incineration.

   D. fluctuation.

**The best answer is A.** Key words from the surrounding text include *collect, become dense, pool,* and *form.* Each of these can be used to describe the process of something accumulating. Choice **B** is a vague word that most nearly means something like *achievement.* While space dust collecting into a huge cloud is quite an event, *actualization* could be used to describe a variety of other events and is therefore not a very specific word. The final choices are better, but there is no evidence in the paragraph of anything heating up (**C**), and the passage makes no mention of anything changing back and forth (**D**).

2. **The main idea of the last paragraph (lines 43–47) is that:**
   F. it takes a long time for a star to form.

   G. some nebulae take millions of years to form; some take trillions.

   H. the death of an old star may begin the life of a new one.

   J. stars must die just as people must die.

**The best answer is H.** The paragraph describes the possibility of a dying star forming a new nebula. **F** and **G** are factual details used to qualify this idea, while **J** is a supporting detail used to relate the idea to our conditions on earth.

3. **At what stage is our sun?**
   A. planetary nebula stage

   B. protostar stage

   C. main sequence stage

   D. red giant stage

**The best answer is C.** This answer is stated in the third paragraph.

Copyright © American Book Company. DO NOT DUPLICATE. 1-888-264-5877.

4. **Which sequence best describes that of our sun?**

    **F.** protostar, main sequence star, white dwarf star, red giant star

    **G.** protostar, main sequence star, red giant star, white dwarf star

    **H.** dwarf star, main sequence star, red giant star, protostar

    **J.** main sequence star, protostar, red giant star, white dwarf star

**The best answer is G.** This is the process described in paragraphs three through five. If the sequence isn't clear, read the passage again and note each indication of a new step.

5. **Approximately what percentage of a nebula consists of helium?**

    **A.** ninety-seven percent

    **B.** three percent or less

    **C.** ninety percent or more

    **D.** It is impossible to estimate.

**The best answer is B.** Since a nebula's contents are "ninety-seven percent hydrogen," helium could only make up, at maximum, the remaining three percent. This rules out **A** and **C**. **D** is also incorrect; while it may be difficult to know something for sure, it is very rarely impossible to estimate something. To *estimate* means to make a guess based on available evidence.

6. **Compared to the protostar stage, the main sequence stage:**

    I. produces more light.

    II. lasts longer.

    III. marks the beginning of fusion.

    **F.** I only

    **G.** III only

    **H.** I and II only

    **J.** II and III only

**The best answer is H.** Roman numerals I and II are supported by phrases from the third paragraph like "increases its luminosity" and "makes up ninety percent of a normal star's lifetime," respectively. III inverts the order of events; it is fusion that marks the beginning of the main sequence stage, not the other way around.

Copyright © American Book Company. DO NOT DUPLICATE. 1-888-264-5877.

7. **Compared to a white dwarf star, a black dwarf star:**

   I. is cooler.

   II. has a larger core mass.

   III. is at a later stage.

   **A.** I only

   **B.** III only

   **C.** I and II only

   **D.** I and III only

**The best answer is D.** In line 32, it is stated that a white dwarf theoretically "cools into" a black dwarf. This means both I and III are correct. There is no support for II in the passage.

8. **Which of the following does NOT lead to a supernova?**

   **F.** Atoms collapsing.

   **G.** A white dwarf is formed.

   **H.** Star core can no longer support its own mass.

   **J.** Star core becomes larger than 1.4 times as massive as the sun.

**The best answer is G.** According to the fifth paragraph, a white dwarf's formation is the outcome produced by the death of a star of less than 1.4 solar masses. White dwarfs and supernovas are alternatives to each other, not steps in the same process. Choices **F**, **H**, and **J** are each a part of the formation of a supernova and thus do not answer the question.

9. **Why is our sun more luminous than most of its neighboring stars?**

   I. It is younger.

   II. It is larger.

   III. It is a red giant.

   **A.** I only

   **B.** II only

   **C.** III only

   **D.** I and II only

**The best answer is A.** Lines 19–20 both support Roman numeral I and negate II. The last sentence of the fourth paragraph implies that our star isn't a red giant yet.

Copyright © American Book Company. DO NOT DUPLICATE. 1-888-264-5877.

**10.** **Just before the fusion process of a star ends, what takes place?**

    **F.**  The star contracts.

    **G.**  The outer layers cool.

    **H.**  The color shifts to a reddish tone.

    **J.**  The core begins to form iron.

**The best answer is J.** The end of the fusion process is clearly detailed in the fourth paragraph. The other choices reference events that occur after fusion ends.

## CHAPTER 7 SUMMARY

**Natural sciences** passages focus on the content areas of anatomy, astronomy, biology, botany, chemistry, ecology, geology, medicine, meteorology, microbiology, natural history, physiology, physics, technology, or zoology.

The **special traits** of natural science passages:

- **various subjects**
- **scientific method**
- **formal language**
- **lack of bias**
- **straightforward**

Copyright © American Book Company. DO NOT DUPLICATE. 1-888-264-5877.

# CHAPTER 7 REVIEW

**NATURAL SCIENCE:** This passage was adapted from "Genetically Modified Foods" (©2008 American Book Company).

1    Think about the foods in your local supermarket's produce section. Almost all the fruits, vegetables, and grains differ greatly from their wild ancestors
5    in taste and appearance. Humans have been selectively breeding crops to maximize desirable characteristics for at least ten thousand years. Farmers have passed along the idea of breeding
10   the best plants together to increase production, maximize resistance to disease, and improve nutritional qualities since shortly after the beginning of agriculture.

15   During the last couple of decades, increasing knowledge about DNA has allowed scientists to alter plants in laboratories. Instead of relying on pollination, scientists can insert genes
20   directly into plants. A transgene, or implanted gene containing a desired characteristic, may come from a bacterium, virus, animal, or another plant. Genetically altered crops can
25   also be called transgenic crops. Today, up to 70 percent of all packaged goods in grocery stores contains genetically modified foods. About 70 percent of soybeans and about 25 percent of corn
30   produced in the United States have been genetically modified.

Advocates of genetic modification point out that the introduction of pest-resistant genes into crops greatly
35   reduces the need for potentially dangerous pesticides. Genetic modification also may improve human health, especially in developing
40   regions. Scientists are researching methods to reduce widespread vitamin A deficiency among people in less developed regions of Asia by genetically engineering rice to produce
45   beta-carotene. Since the diet in these countries consists largely of rice, transgenic rice may significantly reduce blindness among poor Asians. Researchers are even looking into
50   producing bananas containing vaccines against diseases like cholera and hepatitis B and ways to prevent cows from transmitting their harmful strain of E. coli.

55   Despite these advances, the topic of genetic modification of food crops is highly debated throughout the world. Many nations have laws strictly regulating the growth and sale of
60   genetically modified foods. Concerns over the effects of genetic modification on humans and ecosystems have sparked widespread debate. Some religious people oppose the idea of
65   "playing God" or altering things that they believe only God should alter. The point at which they think modern science crosses into unethical territory differs, but genetic engineering is a
70   clear boundary for many. Certain Jews and Muslims interpret their religious texts, which forbid the consumption of specific animal meats, to mean that even plants containing the genes of
75   these animals are forbidden. Vegetarians sometimes have similar concerns. In response to these kinds of apprehensions, genetic engineers can only offer assurances that consumers
80   will still have options, a promise that doesn't convince every skeptic.

Copyright © American Book Company. DO NOT DUPLICATE. 1-888-264-5877.

Environmentalists may worry about affecting delicate ecosystems by introducing plants that are more durable than their surroundings. Proponents of engineering would respond to environmental concerns by pointing out things like forests that grow faster and thus take in more carbon dioxide, ferns that consume toxic substances from soil, and crops that need far fewer fertilizers and harmful pesticides. However, modifying nature remains a very complicated matter, and critics have provided a check for overeager engineers on many occasions. For example, Nebraska scientists were halted from engineering local soy with proteins from Brazil nuts because they failed to consider that many people are allergic to nuts. Even more importantly, detractors pointed out that equalizing all members of a population with new traits increases the reach of diseases, as any infection that can affect one member can affect the whole. Other observers fear that genetic engineering may lead to advances like extensive embryonic stem cell research, human genetic engineering, and human cloning.

At least eight government agencies currently attempt to regulate genetically-modified foods in the United States. Some scientists believe that our ever-expanding knowledge of genes and DNA may allow us to one day discover and activate desirable traits that are currently dormant in many of our crops. This technology may render transgenic crops an issue of the past. For now, though, people throughout the world need to make informed decisions about the use of transgenic technology.

Copyright © American Book Company. DO NOT DUPLICATE. 1-888-264-5877.

1. **Based on the third paragraph (lines 33–54), what ailment can a healthy supply of vitamin A protect humans from?**
   A. cholera
   B. E. coli
   C. blindness
   D. poverty

2. **Before scientists had the ability to insert genes directly into plants, humans modified plants in order to obtain the desirable characteristics by:**
   F. using transgenes.
   G. planting transgenic crops.
   H. invoking divine intervention.
   J. controlling the pollination process.

3. **Which word from lines 107–112 best shows the author's perception of human genetic breeding as more controversial than agricultural genetic breeding?**
   A. observers
   B. fear
   C. advances
   D. lead

4. **Which of the following possibilities would most trouble people who are worried about the effects of genetic engineering on ecosystems?**
   F. insects becoming stronger to prey on more durable plants
   G. products with unknown allergens being sold in grocery stores
   H. lack of sufficient critical pesticides
   J. offending large numbers of Jews and Muslims

5. **As used in line 96, the word *check* most nearly means:**

   A. restraint.

   B. payment.

   C. quick look.

   D. stoppage.

6. **The main idea of the second paragraph (lines 15–32) is that:**

   F. a transgene may come from another plant or from a bacterium, virus, or animal.

   G. up to 70 percent of all packaged goods in grocery stores contain genetically modified foods.

   H. increasing knowledge about DNA has allowed scientists to alter plants in laboratories.

   J. genetically altered crops can also be called transgenic crops.

7. **Based on the fourth paragraph (lines 55–81), one concern about genetic engineering that vegetarians raise is the possibility of:**

   A. excessive amounts of vitamin A.

   B. expensive food in the produce section.

   C. introducing hepatitis B to poor regions.

   D. animal DNA being used in plants.

8. **Trees engineered to grow at a quicker rate are able to:**

   F. soak up toxic substances from soil.

   G. absorb more carbon dioxide.

   H. flourish without fertilizers.

   J. resist disease due to genetic diversity.

9. **Which of these is the best example of a transgenic crop?**

   A. high-quality wheat able to mature despite heavy rains

   B. soy adapted to its environment by growing in long vines

   C. corn genetically modified to use sunlight more efficiently

   D. varieties of rice, found in Asia, containing very little vitamin A

10. **It can be reasonably inferred from lines 26–28, "up to 70 percent of all packaged goods in grocery stores contain genetically modified foods," that:**

    F. 70 percent foods include an ingredient that has been genetically modified.

    G. 70 percent of foods have been entirely genetically modified.

    H. 70 percent of the genes of most plants have been modified.

    J. 70 percent of grocery stores package their own goods.

Copyright © American Book Company. DO NOT DUPLICATE. 1-888-264-5877.

# ACT Reading
# Practice Test One

35 Minutes—40 Questions

**DIRECTIONS:** There are four passages in this test. Each passage is followed by ten questions. After reading a passage, choose the best answer to each question. You may refer to the passages as often as necessary.

Copyright © American Book Company. DO NOT DUPLICATE. 1-888-264-5877.

**Passage I**

**PROSE FICTION:** This passage is adapted from "I Went Back to Mars" by Michael Kabel (©2007 American Book Company). John is the narrator of the story.

1    I'd saved for months, but the best passage I could afford went only so far as the supply station above Meroe Patera, a dilapidated wagon-wheel
5    model from two hundred years ago that was, incredibly, still in use. Stepping off the liner and through its airlock was like walking back in time: the scrubbed air might as well have twinkled with
10   the dust that floated in real sunlight back home.

     Commuter shuttles, the ticket agent back home had promised me, left for the surface every two hours. A
15   terminal at the farthest end of one spoke told me the schedule had been cut back to twice daily, even going so far as to blame the economic troubles on the system-wide recession. I went
20   back to the station's central hub and the ring of calling booths at its center. At one time the area might have looked like an urban plaza or seaside park. Now the plastic flower boxes were
25   empty and the trees had dropped dead leaves to the ceramic floor.

     Of all the old names, only Halbursham still had a listed number. He broke out in a grin as his face came
30   on the screen.

     "Well, well, well," he said laughing. "How you been, Johnny?"

     His smile faded when I told him where I was. "You're really in orbit?"

35   I poked at the screen. On his end, it would look like I was trying to tap his forehead. "I can't really explain right now," I said. "This thing's expensive."

     "Of course." He glanced at
40   something off to one side. "There's a cargo truck coming up in a bit. I'll set you up to hitch a ride."

     Two hours later the truck's pilot strapped me into a rear cockpit couch
45   and fired the maneuvering jets. The station fell away from us, the craft rotating towards the murky red and blue swirls of Mars. As we turned, I remembered my childhood fear of
50   elevators and closed my eyes, dreading the sensation of waiting for a halt that never comes. At the end of the drop, I would imagine landing on springs, or steel cables above me pulling taut. So I
55   wasn't paying attention as we descended toward the dark soil of the Elysium Plain.

     Halbursham waited for me on the runway, fatter since I'd been gone and
60   with deep rings around his eyes smudged with red dust.

     We hugged just like old friends. "What have you been doing with yourself?" he asked.

65   "I'm a security analyst back on Earth," I said, trying to sound proud of myself. "At the space museum in New New Orleans."

     "I know what you're doing here,"
70   he said. "You've come back for Kyla, haven't you?"

     I looked away. There were rain clouds above the volcanic hills to the east. "The court's agreed to a hearing."

75   "Forget about them," he said. "How did you persuade her mother?"

Copyright © American Book Company. DO NOT DUPLICATE. 1-888-264-5877.

It had taken months to even get my ex-wife to respond to my letters. "She wouldn't pass this up."

80    Halbursham led me to the motor pool and put a key fob in my hand. "Follow the old railroad, out to the Syrtis valleys," he said. "You can't miss her husband's place."

85    When I tried to thank him, he walked off. "Best of luck to you, John." he said.

I called Lyssa from the phone inside the dirty spaceport. Her new
90    husband answered the phone.

"She took Kyla out for a walk," he said before I'd spoken. His face had the pinkish hue that is a kind of tan there, and his hair was neatly combed despite
95    the winds. "They'll be back within the half-hour."

I told him I'd be stopping by before heading on to a hotel in Kennedy City.

"You're welcome to stay with us,"
100   he said calmly. "You've come a long way, and it's stupid to run back and forth after that."

The kindness made me think before speaking. "Thanks just the same."

105   Halbursham insisted on loaning me a jeep, a fairly new model with tires threaded like a screw. At the gates, a throng of squatters milled about, their shoulders stooped and their backs
110   hunched, almost certainly from working off their emigration passage in some ore foundry under one of the mountains. Entire families stood or huddled against the fence, some not
115   taking their eyes off the sky to notice the jeep coming within inches of running them down. They were still

looking up as I turned onto the highway, hypnotized by their own
120   hopes of escape floating out in the ruddy sky.

1.  As it is used in line 4, *dilapidated* most nearly means:

A. growing old.

B. falling apart.

C. injured.

D. damaged.

2.  The author's main point in describing the space station is to show that:

F. not everyone wants to explore Mars.

G. Mars is a more hostile planet than anyone had realized.

H. the narrator doesn't want to be there.

J. not everything in the future will remain brand new.

3.  As it is used in line 119, *hypnotized* most nearly means:

A. delighted.

B. oblivious.

C. preoccupied.

D. thrilled.

4.  According to the passage, why has the narrator most likely returned to Mars?

F. for custody of his child

G. to find a better-paying job

H. in search of revenge

J. just following orders

Copyright © American Book Company. DO NOT DUPLICATE. 1-888-264-5877.

5. From the information provided in the passage, all of the following can be inferred about the Martian colonies EXCEPT:

   A. conditions on Mars will eventually get better.

   B. people came to Mars trying to find a better life.

   C. the colonies were once in better shape economically.

   D. life on Mars is hard and uncompromising.

6. The words "shoulders stooped" in line 109 convey the degree to which:

   F. the travelers feel optimistic about getting on a spaceship.

   G. everyone hurries to get out of the narrator's way.

   H. colonists have endured hard labor since coming to Mars.

   J. the people feel incapable of getting inside the spaceport.

7. The narrator's tone in the passage can best be described as one of:

   A. self-pity.

   B. sadness.

   C. anger.

   D. regret.

8. The phrase in lines 83–84 "you can't miss her husband's place," which indirectly describes Lyssa's new husband, contrasts with the indirect description of the narrator in which of the following phrases:

   F. "…I said, trying to sound proud of myself"

   G. "I remembered my childhood fear of elevators and closed my eyes"

   H. "thanks just the same"

   J. "the best passage I could afford went only so far as…"

9. It can be inferred that, since leaving Mars, the narrator:

   A. has kept close ties with old friends and family.

   B. longs to live on Mars once again.

   C. has struggled with money and a new career.

   D. forgot why he left in the first place.

10. According to the passage, why doesn't the narrator pay attention as the ship descends toward Elysium Plain?

    F. He's distracted by the murky red and blue swirls of Mars.

    G. He is preoccupied with thoughts of his ex-wife.

    H. He's thinking about how he is two hours late.

    J. He dreads the sensation of flying in space.

Copyright © American Book Company. DO NOT DUPLICATE. 1-888-264-5877.

## Passage II

**SOCIAL SCIENCE:** This passage is
adapted from *Mark Twain: A Biography—
The Personal and Literary Life of Samuel
Langhorne Clemens* by Albert Bigelow
Paine. The American writer Samuel Clemens
is better known by his pen name  Mark
Twain.

1    On page 492 of the old volume of
Suetonius, which Mark Twain read
until his very last day, there is a
reference to one Flavius Clemens, a
5    man of wide repute "for his want of
energy," and in a marginal note he has
written:

"I guess this is where our line
starts."

10    It was like him to write that. It
spoke in his whimsical fashion the
attitude of humility, the ready
acknowledgment of shortcoming,
which was his chief characteristic and
15    made him lovable—in his personality
and in his work.

Historically, we need not accept
this identity of the Clemens ancestry.
The name itself has a kindly meaning,
20    and was not an uncommon one in
Rome. There was an early pope by that
name, and it appears now and again in
the annals of the Middle Ages. More
lately there was a Gregory Clemens, an
25    English landowner who became a
member of Parliament under Cromwell
and signed the death-warrant of
Charles I. Afterward he was tried as a
regicide, his estates were confiscated,
30    and his head was exposed on a pole on
the top of Westminster Hall.

Tradition says that the family of
Gregory Clemens did not remain in
England, but emigrated to Virginia (or
35    New  Jersey), and from them, in

direct  line, descended the Virginia
Clemenses, including John Marshall
Clemens, the father of Mark Twain.
Perhaps the line could be traced, and its
40    various steps identified, but, after all,
an ancestor more or less need not
matter when it is the story of a
descendant that is to be written.

Of Mark Twain's immediate
45    forebears, however, there is something
to be said. His paternal grandfather,
whose name also was Samuel, was a
man of culture and literary taste. In
1797 he married a Virginia girl, Pamela
50    Goggin; and of their five children John
Marshall Clemens, born August 11,
1798, was the eldest—becoming male
head of the family at the age of seven,
when his father was accidentally killed
55    at a house-raising. The family was not
a poor one, but the boy grew up with a
taste for work. As a youth he became a
clerk in an iron manufactory, at
Lynchburg, and doubtless studied at
60    night. At all events, he acquired an
education, but injured his health in the
mean time, and somewhat later, with
his mother and the younger children,
removed to Adair County, Kentucky,
65    where the widow presently married a
sweetheart of her girlhood, one Simon
Hancock, a good man. In due course,
John Clemens was sent to Columbia,
the county seat, to study law.

70    This was in 1821. John Clemens
was now a young man of twenty-three,
never very robust, but with a good
profession, plenty of resolution, and a
heart full of hope and dreams. Sober,
75    industrious, and unswervingly upright,
it seemed certain that he must make his
mark. That he was likely to be
somewhat too optimistic, even
visionary, was not then regarded as a
80    misfortune.

It was two years later that he met
Jane Lampton; whose mother was a
Casey—a Montgomery-Casey whose
father was of the Lamptons (Lambtons)
85   of Durham, England, and who on her
own account was reputed to be the
handsomest girl and the wittiest, as
well as the best dancer, in all Kentucky.
The Montgomery and Casey annals
90   were full of blood-curdling adventures,
and there is today a Casey County next
to Adair, with a Montgomery County
somewhat farther east. As for the
Lamptons, there is an earldom in the
95   English family, and there were
claimants even then in the American
branch. All these things were worth
while in Kentucky, but it was rare Jane
Lampton herself—buoyant and
100  celebrated for her beauty and her grace;
able to dance all night, and all day too,
for that matter—that won the heart of
John Marshall Clemens, swept him off
his feet almost at the moment of their
105  meeting. Many of the characteristics
that made Mark Twain famous were
inherited from his mother. His sense of
humor, his prompt, quaintly spoken
philosophy, these were distinctly her
110  contribution to his fame. Speaking of
her in a later day, he once said:

    "She had a sort of ability which is
rare in man and hardly existent in
woman—the ability to say a humorous
115  thing with the perfect air of not
knowing it to be humorous."

11. **Considering the context in which it appears, a *regicide* (line 29) most likely means a person who:**

  A. does not follow regulations.

  B. kills a monarch.

  C. overthrows a ruler.

  D. is a member of Parliament.

12. **What is the main focus of the sixth paragraph (lines 44–69)?**

  F. Twain's grandfather.

  G. Twain's father.

  H. The paternal side of Twain's family.

  J. The maternal side of Twain's family.

13. **In the first paragraph, Flavius Clemens is described as "a man of wide repute 'for his want of energy.'" This most likely means that Flavius Clemens was known for:**

  A. being lazy.

  B. being tired.

  C. being energetic.

  D. being eager to help others.

Copyright © American Book Company. DO NOT DUPLICATE. 1-888-264-5877.

14. Considering the information provided in the passage, which of the following is the most accurate description of the sequence of events taking place before the birth of Mark Twain?

F. John Marshall Clemens is born, Gregory Clemens' family moves to the United States, Samuel Clemens marries Pamela Goggin, Samuel Clemens is killed at a house raising.

G. Gregory Clemens' family moves to the United States, Samuel Clemens marries Pamela Goggin, John Marshall Clemens is born, Samuel Clemens is killed at a house raising.

H. Samuel Clemens marries Pamela Goggin, John Marshall Clemens is born, Gregory Clemens' family moves to the United States, Samuel Clemens is killed at a house raising.

J. Gregory Clemens' family moves to the United States, Samuel Clemens marries Pamela Goggin, Samuel Clemens is killed at a house raising, John Marshall Clemens is born.

15. If Twain received characteristics from both of his parents equally, he would best be described as:

A. scholarly, hard working, determined, and positive.

B. good-looking, funny, lively, and robust.

C. studious, idealistic, funny, and clever.

D. industrious, persistent, righteous, and constrained.

16. How does Twain's quotation about his mother Jane Clemens (lines 112–116) compare to his quotation about his family ancestor Flavius Clemens (lines 5–6)?

I. Twain seem to be ashamed in the quotation about his mother and boastful in the one about his ancestor.

II. In both of Twain's comments, it seems he is apologizing for the faulty characteristics of his family members.

III. Twain's comment in the quotation about Flavius is an example of the ability that he describes in the one about his mother.

F. I only

G. II only

H. III only

J. II and III only

17. According to the eighth paragraph (lines 81–111), what motivated Twain's father, John Marshall Clemens, to marry Jane Lampton?

I. Jane's family background

II. Jane's beauty

III. Jane's grace

A. I only

B. II only

C. II and III only

D. I, II, and III

Copyright © American Book Company. DO NOT DUPLICATE. 1-888-264-5877.

**18. According to the details of the passage, what was most likely the cause of John Marshall Clemens' growing up "with a taste for work" (line 57)?**

I. His family needed the income.

II. He became the head of the family at an early age.

III. His father made him work, and John accepted it.

F. I only

G. II only

H. I and II only

J. I, II, and III

**19. What attitude does the author seem to have toward Mark Twain's family ancestry?**

A. He seems to doubt the authenticity of Twain's family line.

B. He seems boastful about the family's well-documented legacy.

C. He seems embarrassed by the conduct of some of Twain's ancestors.

D. He seems to feel that Twain's immediate forebears had a much greater influence on him than did earlier ancestors.

**20. Judging by the overall tone of the passage, how was the last paragraph (lines 112–116) of the passage most likely meant to be understood by its original readers?**

F. as an insult to women

G. as a compliment to Twain's mother

H. as an inside joke

J. as a criticism of Twain's mother

## Passage III

**HUMANITIES:** This passage is adapted from *Language: An Introduction to the Study of Speech* by Edward Sapir.

1     Speech is so familiar a feature of daily life that we rarely pause to define it. It seems as natural to man as walking, and only less so than
5 breathing. Yet it needs but a moment's reflection to convince us that this naturalness of speech is but an illusory feeling. The process of acquiring speech is, in sober fact, an utterly
10 different sort of thing from the process of learning to walk. In the case of the latter function, culture, in other words, the traditional body of social usage, is not seriously brought into play. The
15 child is individually equipped, by the complex set of factors that we term biological heredity, to make all the needed muscular and nervous adjustments that result in walking.
20 Indeed, the very conformation of these muscles and of the appropriate parts of the nervous system may be said to be primarily adapted to the movements made in walking and in similar
25 activities. In a very real sense the normal human being is predestined to walk, not because his elders will assist him to learn the art, but because his organism is prepared from birth, or
30 even from the moment of conception, to take on all those expenditures of nervous energy and all those muscular adaptations that result in walking. To put it concisely, walking is an inherent,
35 biological function of man.

Copyright © American Book Company. DO NOT DUPLICATE. 1-888-264-5877.

Not so language. It is of course true that in a certain sense the individual is predestined to talk, but that is due entirely to the circumstance that he is born not merely in nature, but in the lap of a society that is certain, reasonably certain, to lead him to its traditions. Eliminate society and there is every reason to believe that he will learn to walk, if, indeed, he survives at all. But it is just as certain that he will never learn to talk, that is, to communicate ideas according to the traditional system of a particular society. Or, again, remove the new-born individual from the social environment into which he has come and transplant him to an utterly alien one. He will develop the art of walking in his new environment very much as he would have developed it in the old. But his speech will be completely at variance with the speech of his native environment. Walking, then, is a general human activity that varies only within circumscribed limits as we pass from individual to individual. Its variability is involuntary and purposeless. Speech is a human activity that varies without assignable limit as we pass from social group to social group, because it is a purely historical heritage of the group, the product of long-continued social usage. It varies as all creative effort varies—not as consciously, perhaps, but none the less as truly as do the religions, the beliefs, the customs, and the arts of different peoples. Walking is an organic, an instinctive, function (not, of course, itself an instinct); speech is a non-instinctive, acquired, "cultural" function.

There is one fact that has frequently tended to prevent the recognition of language as a merely conventional system of sound symbols that has seduced the popular mind into attributing to it an instinctive basis that it does not really possess. This is the well-known observation that under the stress of emotion, say of a sudden twinge of pain or of unbridled joy, we do involuntarily give utterance to sounds that the hearer interprets as indicative of the emotion itself. But there is all the difference in the world between such involuntary expression of feeling and the normal type of communication of ideas that is speech. The former kind of utterance is indeed instinctive, but it is non-symbolic; in other words, the sound of pain or the sound of joy does not, as such, indicate the emotion, it does not stand aloof, as it were, and announce that such and such an emotion is being felt. What it does is to serve as a more or less automatic overflow of the emotional energy; in a sense, it is part and parcel of the emotion itself. Moreover, such instinctive cries hardly constitute communication in any strict sense. They are not addressed to any one, they are merely overheard, if heard at all, as the bark of a dog, the sound of approaching footsteps, or the rustling of the wind is heard. If they convey certain ideas to the hearer, it is only in the very general sense in which any and every sound or even any phenomenon in our environment may be said to convey an idea to the perceiving mind. If the involuntary cry of pain which is conventionally represented by "Oh!" be looked upon as a true speech symbol equivalent to some such idea as "I am in great pain," it is just as allowable to interpret the appearance of clouds as an equivalent symbol that carries the definite message "It is likely to rain." A definition of language, however, that is so extended as to cover every type of inference becomes utterly meaningless.

Copyright © American Book Company. DO NOT DUPLICATE. 1-888-264-5877.

**21. As it is used in line 85, the word *unbridled* most nearly means:**

A. inhibited.

B. casual.

C. unrestrained.

D. disorderly.

**22. The main idea of the first paragraph can best be summarized by using which of these sentences from the passage?**

F. Speech is so familiar a feature of daily life that we rarely pause to define it.

G. The process of acquiring speech is, in sober fact, an utterly different sort of thing from the process of learning to walk.

H. The child is individually equipped, by the complex set of factors that we term biological heredity, to make all the needed muscular and nervous adjustments that result in walking.

J. To put it concisely, walking is an inherent, biological function of man.

**23. The author argues that if society were eliminated, a person:**

A. would still be able to walk and talk.

B. would not be able to walk or talk.

C. would still be able to walk.

D. would still be able to talk.

**24. According to the first paragraph, before a person walks:**

F. he first learns to talk.

G. his body is already equipped for the task.

H. his elders teach him the art of walking.

J. he first learns to crawl.

**25. According to the author, which activity is a cultural function?**

A. walking

B. talking

C. both walking and talking

D. neither walking nor talking

**26. According to the second paragraph, if a child were removed from his social environment and placed in a very different one, what effect would this have upon the way he walks and talks?**

F. The individual would walk and talk differently than he would have in his native environment.

G. The individual would walk and talk just as he would have in his native environment.

H. The individual would walk just as he would in any environment, but he would talk differently than he would have in his native environment.

J. The individual would talk just as he would in any environment, but he would walk differently than he would have in his native environment.

Copyright © American Book Company. DO NOT DUPLICATE. 1-888-264-5877.

27. **According to the third paragraph, if a person cries out in pain after accidentally hitting his finger with a hammer, he is:**

    A. communicating his present emotion to others.

    B. not communicating at all.

    C. communicating to everyone.

    D. communicating his present emotion to himself.

28. **What might the author's critics argue about the instinctive nature of language?**

    I. Automatic expressions of joy or pain are evidence of the instinctive nature of language.

    II. Language is more than a merely conventional system of sound symbols.

    III. The involuntary utterance of sound is a type of communication.

    F. I only

    G. III only

    H. I and II only

    J. I, II, and III

29. **Compared to talking, walking is more closely related to:**

    I. breathing.

    II. crying out in pain.

    III. creating art.

    A. I only

    B. II only

    C. III only

    D. I and II only

30. **In terms of developing the author's overall main idea, the third paragraph of the passage serves to:**

    I. summarize the main points of the first paragraph.

    II. restate the argument established in the second paragraph.

    III. address evidence in popular opinion that may seem contrary to the author's argument.

    F. I only

    G. II only

    H. III only

    J. II and III only

Copyright © American Book Company. DO NOT DUPLICATE. 1-888-264-5877.

## Passage IV

**NATURAL SCIENCE:** This passage is adapted from "Recovering from Acid Rain—Too Late?" (©2008 American Book Company).

1    During our planet's history, many dead plants and animals have become buried together under sediment. Sediment is bits of rock and other
5    matter that pile up over time. The heavy weight of sediment causes intense heat and pressure. Over millions of years, this transforms the remains of these organisms into
10   substances like coal, oil, and natural gas. Humans first began learning how to put these fossil fuels to extensive use about two hundred years ago. The rate of fossil fuel use has been increasing
15   ever since, especially over the last fifty years. The burning of these fuels is a constant part of the modern lifestyle, providing the most common method for traveling, powering buildings, and
20   transporting goods. In fact, over eighty percent of the world's energy comes from burning fossil fuels. Burning these fuels, however, releases all sorts of things into the air, many of them
25   harmful. In addition to carbon dioxide, fossil fuel emissions contain nitrogen and sulfur, which combine with atmospheric oxygen and water to form strong acids. These acids fall to the
30   ground via precipitation.

     Shortly after the Industrial Revolution, a Scottish chemist found that Manchester, England—perhaps the Revolution's heart—had very
35   acidic rain. This implied a connection between pollution and acid rain. Scientists continued to look into it.

     However, most people were not aware of acid rain until newspapers published
40   reports in the 1990s of acid damaging New Hampshire forests. Acid precipitation is particularly widespread in eastern North America and Europe, which have been the most
45   industrialized regions of the world for a long time. These days, most people have heard of acid rain, but many do not understand it. Acid precipitation can take the form of anything from acid
50   snow to acid fog and can be powerful enough to slowly wear down granite statues until they appear to be in the act of melting. Since acid rain is powerful enough to speed up the decay of
55   buildings, imagine the harm it can do to ponds, lakes, and soil.

     According to the pH scale, which measures acidity, neutral substances have a pH level of seven. Distilled
60   water, for example, is a neutral substance. The more acidic a substance is, the lower its pH rating is. Battery acid rates at about zero, and digestive fluids have a pH of about one. Clean
65   precipitation has a pH rating of 5.6. Any rain with a rating lower than 5.6 is considered acid rain. In parts of New England, reports have mentioned rain with pH levels as low as 2.4, which
70   means it is more acidic than lemon juice and vinegar. Rain with pH levels this low can harm plant leaves and slow down photosynthesis, but that is not the full extent of the damage it can do.

75   Acid rain, once it reaches soil, depletes the natural minerals that organisms need to survive. This further harms trees, animals that depend on trees, and creatures that live in the
80   ground. Scientists believe acid rain played a major role in the large-scale damage to about a quarter of

Copyright © American Book Company. DO NOT DUPLICATE. 1-888-264-5877.

Europe's forests during the 1970s and
'80s. Most insects cannot survive acid
85  rain, which also hinders the plants that
depend on insects for pollination.
Animals that live in rivers and ponds
are especially vulnerable to highly
acidic water, for obvious reasons.
90  Acidity levels below five will often kill
fish eggs; levels that are even lower can
kill adult fish. The acidification of
streams and lakes has reduced or
eliminated many freshwater fish
95  species. Acid snow has particularly
affected the fish populations of Canada
and Scandinavia, while acid fog
threatens the wildlife of mountainous
regions. These changes all affect
100 humans, who need edible organisms in
order to survive. Some scientists
suggest acid rain may even cause
cancer, but they have not been able to
prove this.

105     The United States and most other
developed nations have reduced sulfur
emissions during the last thirty years.
As a result of decreased emissions,
precipitation in the eastern United
110 States is less acidic than it was fifteen
years ago. Will the effects of acid rain
revert if sulfur levels continue to fall?
Observations of previously devastated
ecosystems in Ontario suggest that
115 ecosystems may be able to partially
recover as emissions decline. However,
until emissions drop much further, full
recovery is not possible. Efforts to save
energy by reducing electricity usage,
120 car emissions, and industrial pollution
can go a long way toward repairing
harmed ecosystems.

31. As it is used in lines 29–30, the word *precipitation* most nearly means:
   A. a sudden haste.
   B. casting down.
   C. any form of water.
   D. separating a substance from a solution.

32. The main idea of the third paragraph (lines 57–74) is that:
   F. acid rain has a low pH rating.
   G. acid rain has a high pH rating.
   H. the pH scale measures acidity.
   J. pH can harm plants.

33. As it is used in lines 75–77, the word *depletes* most nearly means:
   A. weakens.
   B. exhausts.
   C. reduces.
   D. uses up.

**34.** According to the fourth paragraph, which of the following best describes the sequence of acid rain's effects on the environment?

   **F.** Natural minerals are depleted from the soil, trees and animals are harmed, humans are affected, then acid rain falls.

   **G.** Acid rain falls, natural minerals are depleted from the soil, trees and animals are harmed, then humans are affected.

   **H.** Acid rain falls, trees and animals are harmed, natural minerals are depleted from the soil, then humans are affected.

   **J.** Acid rain falls, humans are affected, natural minerals are depleted from the soil, then trees and animals are harmed.

**35.** According to the passage, acid rain was first noticed:

   I. shortly after the Industrial Revolution.

   II. in the 1990s.

   III. in New Hampshire.

   **A.** I only

   **B.** III only

   **C.** I and III only

   **D.** II and III only

**36.** Compared to adult fish, fish eggs are:

   **F.** not vulnerable to highly acidic water at all.

   **G.** less vulnerable to highly acidic water.

   **H.** more vulnerable to highly acidic water.

   **J.** equally vulnerable to highly acidic water.

**37.** Which of the following would cause the most damage to plant leaves?

   **A.** lemon juice

   **B.** clean precipitation

   **C.** digestive fluids

   **D.** acid rain

**38.** According to the passage, how do fossil fuel emissions contribute to the creation of acid rain?

   I. by releasing carbon dioxide into the air

   II. by releasing nitrogen into the air

   III. by releasing sulfur into the air

   **F.** I only

   **G.** II only

   **H.** II and III only

   **J.** I, II, and III

Copyright © American Book Company. DO NOT DUPLICATE. 1-888-264-5877.

**39. Which of the following could help to reduce the occurrence of acid rain?**

I. reducing electricity usage

II. reducing car emissions

III. reducing industrial pollution

**A.** I only

**B.** I and II only

**C.** II and III only

**D.** I, II, and III

**40. Which of the following statements best describes the contribution of human activity to the formation of acid rain?**

**F.** Throughout recorded history, human activity has contributed to the formation of acid rain.

**G.** Since the Industrial Revolution human activity has contributed to the formation of acid rain.

**H.** For the last fifty years, human activity has contributed to the formation of acid rain.

**J.** Human activity no longer contributes to the formation of acid rain.

Copyright © American Book Company. DO NOT DUPLICATE. 1-888-264-5877.

# ACT READING TEST PRACTICE TEST 1
## EVALUATION CHART

Use the chart below to better focus your study for the ACT Reading Test. Identify the questions you answered incorrectly. Turn to the appropriate chapters, read the explanations, and complete the extra exercises. Review other chapters as needed.

*Note:* Some questions may appear under multiple chapters because those questions require multiple skills.

| Chapter Number | Question Number |
|---|---|
| Chapter 2: Reading for Understanding | 1, 2, 3, 11, 12, 13, 14, 18, 21, 22, 24, 25, 27, 28, 29, 30, 31, 32, 33, 34, 35, 37, 38, 40 |
| Chapter 3: Critical Reading | 4, 5, 6, 7, 8, 9, 10, 13, 15, 16, 17, 18, 19, 20, 23, 26, 27, 28, 29, 30, 36, 39, 40 |
| Chapter 4: Interpreting Prose Fiction Texts | 1–10 |
| Chapter 5: Interpreting Humanities Texts | 21–30 |
| Chapter 6: Interpreting Social Studies Texts | 11–20 |
| Chapter 7: Interpreting Natural Sciences Texts | 31–40 |

Copyright © American Book Company. DO NOT DUPLICATE. 1-888-264-5877.

# ACT Reading
# Practice Test Two

35 Minutes—40 Questions

**DIRECTIONS:** There are four passages in this test. Each passage is followed by ten questions. After reading a passage, choose the best answer to each. You may refer to the passages as often as necessary.

Copyright © American Book Company. DO NOT DUPLICATE. 1-888-264-5877.

## Passage I

**PROSE FICTION:** This passage is adapted from *Pepita Jiménez* by Juan Valera.

1   The dinner at the house of Pepita
Jiménez, which I mentioned to you,
took place three days ago. As she leads
so retired a life, I had not met her
5   before; she seemed to me, in truth, as
beautiful as she is said to be, and I
noticed that her amiability with my
father was such as to give him reason to
hope, at least judging superficially, that
10  she will yield to his wishes in the end,
and accept his hand.

As there is a possibility of her
becoming my stepmother, I have
observed her with attention; she seems
15  to me to be a remarkable woman,
whose moral qualities I am not able to
determine with exactitude. There is
about her an air of calmness and
serenity that may come either from
20  coldness of heart and spirit, with great
self-control and power of calculating
effects, accompanied by little or no
sensibility; or that may, on the other
hand, proceed from the tranquility of
25  her conscience and the purity of her
aspirations, united to the purpose of
fulfilling in this life the duties imposed
upon her by society, while her hopes
are fixed, meantime, upon loftier
30  things, as their proper goal.

What is certain is that, either
because with this woman everything is
the result of calculation, without any
effort to elevate her mind to a higher
35  sphere, or, it may be, because she
blends in perfect harmony the prose of
daily life with the poetry of her
illusions, there is nothing discernible in
her out of tone with her

40  surroundings, although she possesses a
natural distinction of manner that
elevates her above and separates her
from them all.

She does not affect the dress of a
45  provincial, nor does she, on the other
hand, follow blindly the fashions of the
city; she unites both these styles in her
mode of dress in such a manner as to
appear like a lady, but still a lady
50  country-born and country-bred. She
disguises to a great extent, as I think,
the care she takes of her person. There
is nothing about her to betray the use of
cosmetics or the arts of the toilet. But
55  the whiteness of her hands, the color
and polish of her nails, and the grace
and neatness of her attire denote a
greater regard for such matters than
might be looked for in one who lives in
60  a village, and who is said, besides, to
despise the vanities of this world and to
think only of heavenly things.

Her house is exquisitely clean, and
everything in it reveals the most perfect
65  order. The furniture is neither artistic
nor elegant, nor is it, on the other hand,
either pretentious or in bad taste. To
give a poetic air to her surroundings,
she keeps in the rooms and passages, as
70  well as in the garden, a multitude of
plants and flowers. There is not,
indeed, among them any rare plant or
exotic, but her plants and flowers, of
the commonest species here, are tended
75  with extraordinary care.

Canaries in gilded cages enliven
the whole house with their songs. Its
mistress, it is obvious, has need of
living creatures on which to bestow
80  some of her affection; and besides
several maid-servants, that one would
suppose she had selected with care,
since it can not be by mere chance that

85 they are all pretty, she has, after the
fashion of old maids, various animals
to keep her company—a parrot, a little
dog, whose coat is of the whitest, and
two or three cats, so tame and sociable
that they jump up on one in the most
90 friendly manner.

At one end of the principal saloon
is a species of oratory, whose chief
ornament is an *Infant Jesus,* carved in
wood, with red and white cheeks and
95 blue eyes, and altogether quite
handsome. The dress is of white satin,
with a blue cloak full of little golden
stars; and the image is completely
covered with jewels and trinkets. The
100 little altar on which the figure is placed
is adorned with flowers, and around it
are set pots of broom and bay; and on
the altar itself, which is furnished with
steps, a great many wax tapers are kept
105 burning.

When I behold all this I know not
what to think, but for the most part I am
inclined to believe that the widow loves
herself above all things, and that it is
110 for her recreation, and for the purpose
of furnishing her with occasions for the
effusion of this love, that she keeps the
cats, the canaries, the flowers, and even
the *Infant Jesus* itself, which in her
115 secret soul, perhaps does not occupy a
place very much higher than the
canaries and the cats.

1. **The word *provincial* as used in line 45, is a person that would most nearly be described as:**

    A. bigoted.

    B. inward-looking.

    C. unsophisticated

    D. small-minded.

2. **What is the main insight suggested by the second paragraph of the passage?**

    F. The narrator is excited about the possibility of Pepita Jiménez becoming his stepmother.

    G. The narrator is anxious about the possibility of Pepita Jiménez becoming his stepmother.

    H. The narrator has not yet ascertained what kind of woman Pepita Jiménez is.

    J. The narrator already has Pepita Jiménez figured out.

3. **As it is used in line 7, the word *amiability* most nearly means:**

    A. friendliness.

    B. sympathy.

    C. understanding.

    D. etiquette.

Copyright © American Book Company. DO NOT DUPLICATE. 1-888-264-5877.

**4. The first time the narrator meets Pepita Jiménez:**

I. she gives some indication of interest in marrying his father.

II. she comes across to him as a remarkable woman.

III. she invites him to have dinner at her house three days later.

**F.** I only

**G.** II only

**H.** I and II only

**J.** I, II, and III

**5. According to the last paragraph, Pepita Jiménez:**

**A.** seems to be a very religious person.

**B.** seems to have no interest in religion at all.

**C.** seems to be more concerned with her animals than with religion.

**D.** seems just as concerned with her animals as she is with religion.

**6. In the second paragraph, the narrator considers two possible sources of Pepita Jiménez's "air of calmness and serenity." How do the narrator's considerations in the first paragraph compare to his considerations in the last paragraph?**

**F.** The last paragraph confirms that her "air of calmness and serenity" comes from "coldness of heart and spirit…accompanied by little or no sensibility."

**G.** The last paragraph confirms that her "air of calmness and serenity" comes from the "purity of her aspirations…while her hopes are fixed…on loftier things."

**H.** The last paragraph suggests that her love for herself is more likely the source of her "air of calmness and serenity" than what the narrator originally considered.

**J.** The narrator does not seem to be any closer to understanding Pepita Jiménez.

**7. What would best describe the narrator's attitude toward Pepita Jiménez?**

**A.** He is intrigued by her.

**B.** He is disheartened by her.

**C.** He is irritated by her.

**D.** He identifies with her.

Copyright © American Book Company. DO NOT DUPLICATE. 1-888-264-5877.

8.  How does the personal appearance of Pepita Jiménez compare to the appearance of her house?

    I. A great deal of effort seems to be put into both.

    II. Both would be considered "chic."

    III. Neither would be considered "pretentious."

    F.  I only

    G.  I and III only

    H.  II and III only

    J.  I, II, and III

9.  According to the last paragraph, for what purpose does Pepita Jiménez keep cats, canaries, flowers, and an *Infant Jesus*?

    A.  for decoration.

    B.  to show off.

    C.  to entertain others.

    D.  to love.

10. What might be the reason that Pepita Jiménez's maids and animals are mentioned in the same paragraph (lines 76–90)?

    F.  She treats the animals and the maids the same.

    G.  They are both considered to be decoration for the house.

    H.  They both keep her company.

    J.  Their mention in the same paragraph seems unintentional.

Copyright © American Book Company. DO NOT DUPLICATE. 1-888-264-5877.

## Passage II

**SOCIAL SCIENCE:** This passage is adapted from "The History of the Women's Liberation Movement" (©2007 American Book Company).

1     The *feminist* or *women's liberation movement* was a social and political movement that sought equality of rights and societal status for women.
5     Key goals of this movement included giving women the freedom to choose their own careers and increased freedom to determine their own lifestyles. The history of the women's
10  rights movement goes back to the 1840s, when activists such as Elizabeth Stanton, Susan B. Anthony, and Lucretia Mott advocated equal rights. Few were willing to accept the radical
15  changes suggested by Stanton and Anthony, particularly Stanton's notion that laws that facilitated an inferior position for women were inherently unjust. Views, like that of Catherine
20  Beecher, accepting that a woman's sphere was in the domestic realm but that women should still receive an education, had more general appeal.

    Shortly after World War I, the
25  movement was able to achieve the aim at the forefront of its concerns— suffrage, or "the vote"—with the passing of the Nineteenth Amendment to the U.S. Constitution. Gaining
30  access to the ballot-box would put women in a position to make other changes over time, but the most radical of the advances would be ushered in side-by-side with the civil rights
35  movement.

    In the 1960s, the push for women's rights largely grew from the grass-roots level, but new laws and policies also had a profound impact. At the
40  suggestion of Esther Peterson, director of the Women's Bureau of the Department of Labor, President John F. Kennedy set up the first national Commission on the Status of Women in
45  1962. The following year, the commission reported epidemic employment discrimination, unequal pay, legal inequality, and insufficient enforcement mechanisms for working
50  women with grievances. The commission's report led to the Equal Pay Act of 1963, which made it illegal to pay lesser wages to a woman doing the same work as a man. The new law
55  had limited effect, however, because most women remained in traditionally female occupations that offered low wages and few opportunities for advancement. In 1963, women were
60  paid, on average, 41 percent less than men. Title VII of the Civil Rights Act of 1964 prohibited employment discrimination based on gender, race, color, or ethnic origin. The act also
65  established the Equal Employment Opportunity Commission (EEOC) to enforce the new law.

    Noted feminist Betty Friedan presented the results of her research on
70  American women in a book entitled *The Feminine Mystique* (1963). Friedan's book presented the interesting finding that housewives were not the happy and completely
75  satisfied homemakers portrayed in magazines and television. In 1966, she helped found the National Organization of Women (NOW) and served as its first president. NOW
80  promotes the equality of men and

Copyright © American Book Company. DO NOT DUPLICATE. 1-888-264-5877.

women through legislation, rallies,
marches, and support for like-minded
political candidates. Gloria Steinem, a
journalist and publisher, became a
85  leader in the feminist movement in the
late 1960s. With Betty Friedan and
Shirley Chisholm (the first black
woman elected to Congress), Steinem
helped found the National Women's
90  Political Caucus (1971) to encourage
women to seek political office and to
work for women's rights laws. Friedan,
Steinem, and NOW supported a new
amendment to the Constitution, the
95  Equal Rights Amendment (ERA),
which would have guaranteed women
equal rights. Congress passed the ERA
in 1972 and extended the deadline for
states' ratification by three years. The
100 amendment failed to be ratified by
enough states and was never added to
the US Constitution.

Many of the same people who
mourned the death of the Equal Rights
105 Amendment, however, cheered the
Supreme Court's decision in the case of
*Roe v. Wade*. Gaining the right to
terminate pregnancies was seen by
many as an important step to freeing
110 women from the obligation of being a
mother and from being economically
dependent on men. Prior to 1973, states
could outlaw or restrict abortions
during a woman's pregnancy if they so
115 wished. Citing the right to privacy, the
Supreme Court ruled state laws
restricting a woman's fundamental
right to an abortion during the first
three months of pregnancy to be
120 unconstitutional. Over thirty years
later, *Roe v. Wade* remains one of the
most controversial decisions in US
history.

11. **Based on information in the passage, the title of the book *The Feminine Mystique* (line 71) most likely implied:**
A. that no one really understood women.
B. that the American culture possessed an idealized image of femininity.
C. that women were unable to express their femininity.
D. that women were unsure about why they were unhappy in a domestic role.

12. **The main idea of this passage is:**
F. the growth of the Civil Rights Movement.
G. the struggle for equal pay for women.
H. efforts by the government to curb women's rights.
J. the history of the women's liberation movement.

13. **According to the passage, all of the following were goals of the women's rights movements EXCEPT**
A. the right to vote.
B. the freedom to select their own careers.
C. the right to run for public office.
D. the right to equal pay.

Copyright © American Book Company. DO NOT DUPLICATE. 1-888-264-5877.

14. **According to the passage, which of the following came before the Equal Pay Act of 1963?**

    I. a revealing report by the Commission on the Status of Women

    II. the establishment of the Equal Employment Opportunity Commission

    III. the publishing of Betty Friedan's *The Feminine Mystique* and the founding of the National Organization of Women

    F. I only

    G. III only

    H. I and III only

    J. I, II, and III

15. **According to the passage, compared to Catherine Beecher, Elizabeth Stanton was considered to be:**

    A. more extreme in her views.

    B. more passive in her views.

    C. more realistic in her views.

    D. more uncompromising in her views.

16. **According to the passage, the National Women's Political Caucus was founded to:**

    I. encourage women to seek political office.

    II. work for women's rights laws.

    III. pass the Equal Rights Amendment.

    F. I only

    G. III only

    H. I and II only

    J. I, II, and III

17. **Compared to the other goals of women's liberation, which one was considered to be the most important because it would make way for other changes over time?**

    A. the right to abortion

    B. the right to equal wages

    C. the right to free speech

    D. the right to vote

18. **According to the passage, which of the following did NOT result from the decision of *Roe v. Wade*?**

    F. Many women felt they'd gained freedom from the obligation to become mothers.

    G. States continued to outlaw first-trimester abortions.

    H. Many women experienced a sense of economic independence from men.

    J. There was widespread disagreement over the court's decision.

19. **From the passage, we can infer that the women's right movement has:**

    A. grown little by little in the country's history.

    B. never really gained popular support.

    C. quickly become an antiquated way of thinking.

    D. has already reached all its goals.

Copyright © American Book Company. DO NOT DUPLICATE. 1-888-264-5877.

20. **Based on the passage, we can infer that the prominent figures of the women's movement in the 1840s:**

I. had differing ideas of the roles of women in society.

II. held beliefs that were representative of all women at that time.

III. believed that women should be able to receive an education.

F. I only

G. II only

H. I and III

J. I, II, and III

## Passage III

**HUMANITIES:** This passage is adapted from "Two Tales of Descent" by Dennis Martin (©2008 American Book Company). It is a comparison of the novella *Heart of Darkness* and the movie *Apocalypse Now.*

1      In 1902, Joseph Conrad wrote his acclaimed novella *Heart of Darkness*, a tale about the travels of a steamboat operator, Charlie Marlow, whose job it
5    is to travel far up the Congo River and into the heart of deepest and darkest Africa—all in search of ivory and a company man whose methods of procurement had become quite
10   unsound.

       In 1979, Francis Ford Coppola released his movie *Apocalypse Now,* which was loosely based on Conrad's novel. The main plot line is the same in
15   the movie as it is in the book, complete with the same name for the person who was being sought—Kurtz. The setting is also a river that leads far from civilization and to a more feral and
20   primordial world; the plot shifts from

the madness of British colonization in the Congo to the insanity of the Vietnam War. Settings, scenes, characters, events, and points of view
25   from the book are nearly duplicated in the movie.

       In the novel, we see and hear everything through Charlie Marlow, a restless man who longs to travel
30   somewhere he has never been and who gets far more than he ever bargained for. In the movie, the Marlow figure is Captain Willard, a Green Beret assassin who has been given the assignment to
35   "terminate Colonel Kurtz with extreme prejudice." They both leave the fetters of civilization to travel far up a foreboding river and seemingly back in time into the psyche of the primordial
40   mind.

       As Marlow travels up the Congo River to the main ivory trading station, he feels like he is going back in time. The jungle transforms him; he feels
45   primal, small, and very lost. The further from civilization he goes, the more wild and untamed the landscape becomes, the more savage the inhabitants become, more unrestrained,
50   more pre-human. For Marlow, his point of departure from any structure of civilization is the main trading station. His search for Kurtz after that point lies both in regions of unknown wilderness
55   and in a sense of doom. The same is true for Captain Willard in the movie. He too feels the jungle's mesmerizing powers after his gunboat leaves the confines of Nha Trang harbor and
60   begins the winding trip into the interior.

       Both Marlow and Willard feel repelled by their managers and officers and pulled in by the jungle. They both are seeking Kurtz, a man whom society

Copyright © American Book Company. DO NOT DUPLICATE. 1-888-264-5877.

65  believes to be guilty of using unsound methods without any decent restraint. The battle for both Marlow and Willard is to keep their sanity in the face of untold horrors. Willard fights the
70  insanity that surrounds him on the river, and both men feel themselves becoming more and more like the man they seek, each knowing that the person who was sent up the river on this
75  mission before them ended up dead. Marlow sees his Kurtz as a man whose mind is sane but whose soul is mad, while Willard sees his Kurtz as a man who has "gotten off the boat"—a man
80  who has "split with the whole program."

Both Marlow and Willard finally find their Kurtz deep in the jungle, camped in a tribal setting, surrounded
85  by poles with the heads of dead men on them. Marlow and Willard both observe that those who surround Kurtz worship him, and after seeing Kurtz's use of terror, both Marlow and Willard
90  realize that to a civilized eye, the practices of Kurtz are indeed unsound. "Are my methods unsound?" Colonel Kurtz asks Captain Willard. Looking about him at the heads of men on poles,
95  Willard replies, "I don't see any method at all, sir."

In especially dark scenes, the Kurtz characters in the book and the movie both die and are buried in the jungle. Captain Willard says, "Even the
100  jungle wanted him dead, and that's who he really took his orders from anyway." The last words of both characters are "…the horror…the horror!" By the end of the journey, both Marlow and
105  Willard know what horror really is. They realize that horror comes from the darkest core of our being. It is what is left after we throw off all the illusions and comforts of civilization—a
110  tremendous emptiness. It is the darkness: the unidentifiable paranoia that conceals savage acts and dwells far from the light of civilized action.

**21. As it is used in line 20, the word _primordial_ most nearly means:**

   A. contemporary.

   B. primitive.

   C. wild.

   D. prim.

**22. The main point of the fourth paragraph is that:**

   F. Marlow feels like he is going back in time.

   G. The jungle has a profound impact on both Marlow and Willard.

   H. The jungle is a symbol of what Kurtz has become.

   J. The travels of both Marlow and Willard up the Congo River change their lives.

**23. As it is used in line 38, the word _foreboding_ most nearly means:**

   A. dark.

   B. ominous.

   C. dirty.

   D. promising.

Copyright © American Book Company. DO NOT DUPLICATE. 1-888-264-5877.

**24. Marlow and Willard begin to experience changes within themselves:**

F. after Kurtz has died.

G. when they meet Kurtz face to face.

H. as they are traveling to meet Kurtz.

J. as soon as they are given the assignment to find Kurtz.

**25. All of the following are evidence of Kurtz's personality EXCEPT:**

A. Kurtz being surrounded by poles with the heads of dead men on them.

B. those surrounding Kurtz worshipping him.

C. Kurtz's living in a tribal setting.

D. Kurtz being buried in the jungle.

**26. According to the passage, all of the following impact the change in both Marlow and Willard EXCEPT:**

F. feelings of repulsion from those in authority.

G. an interest in whether their mission will fail or succeed.

H. the impression that the hunter is becoming like the hunted.

J. the sense of being drawn toward the jungle.

**27. According to the conclusion of the passage, horror is the result of:**

I. being disconnected from civilization.

II. embracing death.

III. the darkness within a person.

A. I only

B. I and II only

C. I and III only

D. I, II, and III

**28. *Heart of Darkness* and *Apocalypse Now* hold all of the following in common EXCEPT:**

F. an antagonist of the same name.

G. a wartime setting.

H. the story of a voyage up a river.

J. a hero who undergoes internal change.

**29. As it is described in the passage, *Apocalypse Now* is:**

A. an updated adaptation of *Heart of Darkness*.

B. a loosely-based remake of *Heart of Darkness*.

C. a faithful reproduction of *Heart of Darkness*.

D. a new and improved retelling of *Heart of Darkness*.

Copyright © American Book Company. DO NOT DUPLICATE. 1-888-264-5877.

**30. In terms of developing the main idea of the passage, the second paragraph serves to:**

I. introduce the topic as a comparison.

II. develop the details of the novel.

III. introduce the movie.

**F.** I only

**G.** II only

**H.** I and III only

**J.** I, II, and III

**Passage IV**

**NATURAL SCIENCE:** This passage is adapted from "Geothermal Power" (©2008 American Book Company).

1    Geothermal energy refers to the heat located deep inside the earth. This heat continuously flows outward from the earth's core. When temperatures
5  and pressures become high enough, some mantle rock melts, becoming magma. This magma rises, moving slowly up toward the earth's crust, carrying heat further upward. Usually,
10  magma remains below the earth's crust, heating nearby rock and rainwater that has seeped deep into the earth— sometimes as hot as 700 degrees Fahrenheit. Some of this hot
15  superheated water reaches the earth's surface as hot springs or geysers, but most of it stays deep underground. This natural collection of hot water is called a geothermal reservoir.

20    Engineers can drill wells into reservoirs to bring hot water to the surface. Once hot water and steam travel up these wells, they can be used

to generate electricity in geothermal
25  power plants. Steam, heat, and hot water from reservoirs provide force, which spins the plant's turbine generators and produces electricity. Used water is then returned down an
30  injection well into the reservoir to be reheated, to maintain pressure, and to sustain the reservoir.

    What is the environmental impact of geothermal energy? The impact is
35  usually a positive one. The greatest advantage is that it is very clean. Geothermal power plants do not manufacture steam or smoke by burning any fuels. Generating
40  electricity with hot, underground water helps to conserve nonrenewable fossil fuels. Decreasing the use of these fuels also reduces emissions, thereby preventing damage to the atmosphere.
45  In fact, some geothermal plants are built in the middle of farms, towns, and forests, sharing land with cattle, people, and local wildlife. For ten years, Lake County, California, has
50  been home to five geothermal electric power plants. It is the first and only county in California to meet the strictest air quality standards in the United States.

55    The use of geothermal energy for electricity has grown worldwide to about 7,000 megawatts in twenty-one countries around the world. The United States annually produces about 2,900
60  megawatts of electricity from geothermal energy, comparable to transporting and burning sixty million barrels of oil each year. Considering a barrel of oil can be used to make about
65  forty gallons of gas, and each burned gallon of gas releases about twenty

pounds of $CO_2$, these geothermal plants have prevented over forty-five billion pounds of pollutants from

70 reaching the atmosphere.

The land area required for geothermal plants is smaller per megawatt than for almost every other type of power plant. Geothermal plants

75 do not require the damming of rivers or harvesting of forests. There are no mine shafts, tunnels, open pits, waste heaps, or oil spills. They are designed to run twenty-four hours a day, all year. The

80 plant sits on top of its fuel source, so no heavy trucks or ships are needed to transport materials long distances. They can only be interrupted by weather, disasters, or wars if they are

85 directly struck. There are no price shocks, as geothermal power is cheaper and more reliable than burning oil or coal. So why does every community not use geothermal power instead of

90 coal or nuclear? Currently, it is very expensive to drill deep enough into the earth's crust to capture geothermal energy except in regions where the mantle is close to the crust. For the time

95 being, geothermal power is limited to certain locations.

A more affordable source of geothermal power is the Geothermal Heat Pump, a system designed to

100 provide heating and cooling to a single house. About six feet below the surface in the average backyard, the temperature is usually between 45 and 58 degrees. An installed GHP

105 circulates water through pipes that run underground and through the walls of the house. The GHP extracts heat from the house and puts it into the earth in the summer. In the winter, it extracts

110 heat from the earth and puts it into the

house. In the winter, since the underground temperature would still be a brisk 50 degrees or so, a GHP owner would need a gas furnace or electric

115 heat to get rooms to a higher temperature. GHPs require very little electricity and are easy on the environment. In the United States, over 300,000 homes, schools, and other

120 buildings use GHPs. In Klamath Falls, Oregon, GHP pipes have been run under roads and sidewalks to keep ice thawed in the winter. In New Mexico, pipes were laid under vegetable

125 gardens to extend the growing season.

Ever since ancient Native Americans began using the earth's hot steam springs for warmth and cleaning, this resource has been a valuable tool.

130 However, with our modern high oil prices and environmental concerns, geothermal power may be more crucial than ever. Some experts estimate that large networks of geothermal plants,

135 mostly located in the western states, could provide as much as twenty percent of the nation's power.

31. As it is used in line 21, *reservoirs* most nearly means:

A. artificial ponds or lakes of water.

B. receptacles for storing water.

C. underground accumulations of water.

D. reserves of water, stored for future needs.

Copyright © American Book Company. DO NOT DUPLICATE. 1-888-264-5877.

**32. Which of the following best describes the main idea of the fourth paragraph?**

F. Use of geothermal energy has grown.

G. Using geothermal energy is more efficient and cleaner than using energy produced from oil.

H. The United States is the greatest producer of geothermal energy.

J. The United States annually produces about 2,900 megawatts of electricity from geothermal energy.

**33. Which of the following is NOT a key component for geothermal energy production?**

A. rainwater

B. dirt

C. rock

D. magma

**34. Which of the following best describes the steps of geothermal energy usage?**

F. Wells are drilled; force from steam, heat, and hot water spins turbine generators; electricity is produced; then used water is returned to the reservoir.

G. Wells are drilled; used water is returned to the reservoir; force from steam, heat, and hot water spins turbine generators; then electricity is produced.

H. Force from steam, heat, and hot water spins turbine generators; electricity is produced; wells are drilled; then used water is returned to the reservoir.

J. Wells are drilled; used water is returned to the reservoir; electricity is produced; then force from steam, heat, and hot water spins turbine generators.

**35. Lake County, California:**

I. has five geothermal electric power plants.

II. is the only place that has met the strictest US air quality standards.

III. has been using geothermal energy for over a decade.

A. I only

B. II only

C. I and II only

D. I, II, and III

Copyright © American Book Company. DO NOT DUPLICATE. 1-888-264-5877.

36. **Compared to other power plants, geothermal power plants:**

    I. are much less expensive to build.

    II. require that rivers be dammed for water pressure.

    III. do not require long-distance transportation of materials.

    F. I only

    G. III only

    H. I and II only

    J. I, II, and III

37. **Which of the following is a true statement about geothermal energy usage?**

    A. Ancient Native Americans never used geothermal energy.

    B. A large percentage of modern Americans presently use geothermal energy.

    C. Though ancient Native Americans used geothermal energy for warmth and cleaning, modern Americans no longer do.

    D. Ancient Native Americans used geothermal energy for warmth and cleaning, and modern Americans can use it for warmth and cleaning today.

38. **According to the passage, which of the following is NOT a result of geothermal energy use?**

    F. cleaner air and atmosphere

    G. elimination of high cost drilling

    H. reduced pollution and emissions

    J. conservation of fossil fuel

39. **Which of the following would least likely be used to convert geothermal energy into electricity?**

    A. geysers

    B. heat

    C. hot water

    D. steam

40. **According to the passage, a Geothermal Heat Pump:**

    I. circulates water

    II. displaces heat.

    III. generates electricity from geothermal energy.

    F. II only

    G. III only

    H. I and II only

    J. I, II, and III

Copyright © American Book Company. DO NOT DUPLICATE. 1-888-264-5877.

# ACT Reading Test Practice Test 2
## Evaluation Chart

Use the chart below to better focus your study for the ACT Reading Test. Identify the questions you answered incorrectly. Turn to the appropriate chapters, read the explanations, and complete the extra exercises. Review other chapters as needed.

*Note:* Some questions may appear under multiple chapters because those questions require multiple skills.

| Chapter Number | Question Number |
|---|---|
| Chapter 2: Reading for Understanding | 1, 2, 3, 4, 12, 13, 14, 16, 18, 21, 22, 23, 24, 25, 30, 31, 32, 33, 34, 35, 37, 38, 40 |
| Chapter 3: Critical Reading | 4, 5, 6, 7, 8, 9, 10, 11, 15, 16, 17, 18, 19, 20, 25, 26, 27, 28, 29, 36, 38, 39 |
| Chapter 4: Interpreting Prose Fiction Texts | 1–10 |
| Chapter 5: Interpreting Humanities Texts | 21–30 |
| Chapter 6: Interpreting Social Studies Texts | 11–20 |
| Chapter 7: Interpreting Natural Sciences Texts | 31–40 |

Copyright © American Book Company. DO NOT DUPLICATE. 1-888-264-5877.